EYE ON
Art

ART IN
GLASS

by Phyllis Raybin Emert

LUCENT BOOKS

An imprint of Thomson Gale, a part of The Thomson Corporation

THOMSON
★
GALE

Detroit • New York • San Francisco • New Haven, Conn. • Waterville, Maine • London

THOMSON
GALE ™

Dedicated to Larry and the three Ms—Matt, Melissa, and Marc

Special thanks to Silvestra Puente Praino and Delores Bostrom, Reference Librarians, Mahwah Public Library, Mahwah, New Jersey, without whose help this book would not have been possible.

For more information, contact
Lucent Books
27500 Drake Rd.
Farmington Hills, MI 48331-3535
Or you can visit our Internet site at http://www.gale.com

LIBRARY OF CONGRESS CATALOGING-IN-PUBLICATION DATA

Emert, Phyllis Raybin.
  Art in glass / by Phyllis Raybin Emert.
      p. cm. — (Eye on art)
  Includes bibliographical references and index.
  ISBN 978-1-59018-983-2 (hardcover)
  1. Glassware—History. I. Title. II. Series.
  NK5106.E54 2007
  748—dc22
                                          2007010118

ISBN-10:1-59018-983-3
Printed in the United States of America

CONTENTS

Foreword

"Art has no other purpose than to brush aside ... everything that veils reality from us in order to bring us face to face with reality itself."
—French philosopher Henri-Louis Bergson

Some thirty-one thousand years ago, early humans painted strikingly sophisticated images of horses, bison, rhinoceroses, bears, and other animals on the walls of a cave in southern France. The meaning of these elaborate pictures is unknown, although some experts speculate that they held ceremonial significance. Regardless of their intended purpose, the Chauvet-Pont-d'Arc cave paintings represent some of the first known expressions of the artistic impulse.

From the Paleolithic era to the present day, human beings have continued to create works of visual art. Artists have developed painting, drawing, sculpture, engraving, and many other techniques to produce visual representations of landscapes, the human form, religious and historical events, and countless other subjects. The artistic impulse also finds expression in glass, jewelry, and new forms inspired by new technology. Indeed, judging by humanity's prolific artistic output throughout history, one must conclude that the compulsion to produce art is an inherent aspect of being human, and the results are among humanity's greatest cultural achievements: masterpieces such as the architectural marvels of ancient Greece, Michelangelo's perfectly rendered statue *David*, Vincent van Gogh's visionary painting *Starry Night*, and endless other treasures.

The creative impulse serves many purposes for society. At its most basic level, art is a form of entertainment or the means for a satisfying or pleasant aesthetic experience. But art's true power lies not in its potential to entertain and delight but in its ability to enlighten, to reveal the truth, and by doing so to uplift the human spirit and transform the human race.

One of the primary functions of art has been to serve religion. For most of Western history, for example, artists were paid by the church to produce works with religious themes and subjects. Art was thus a tool to help human beings transcend mundane, secular reality and achieve spiritual enlightenment. One of the best-known, and largest-scale, examples of Christian religious art is the Sistine Chapel in the Vatican in Rome. In 1508 Pope Julius II commissioned Italian Renaissance artist Michelangelo to paint the chapel's vaulted ceiling, an area of 640 square yards (535 sq. m). Michelangelo spent four years on scaffolding, his neck craned, creating a panoramic fresco of some three hundred human figures. His paintings depict Old Testament prophets and heroes, sibyls of Greek mythology, and nine scenes from the Book of Genesis, including the Creation of Adam, the Fall of Adam and Eve from the Garden of Eden, and the Flood. The ceiling of the Sistine Chapel is considered one of the greatest works of Western art and has inspired the awe of countless Christian pilgrims and other religious seekers. As eighteenth-century German poet and author Johann Wolfgang von Goethe wrote, "Until you have seen this Sistine Chapel, you can have no adequate conception of what man is capable of."

In addition to inspiring religious fervor, art can serve as a force for social change. Artists are among the visionaries of any culture. As such, they often perceive injustice and wrongdoing and confront others by reflecting what they see in their work. One classic example of art as social commentary was created in May 1937, during the brutal Spanish civil war. On May 1 Spanish artist Pablo Picasso learned of the recent attack on the small Basque village of Guernica by German airplanes allied with fascist forces led by Francisco Franco. The German pilots had used the village for target practice, a three-hour bombing that killed sixteen hundred civilians. Picasso, living in Paris, channeled his outrage over the massacre into his painting *Guernica*, a black, white, and gray mural that depicts dismembered animals and fractured human figures whose faces are contorted in agonized expressions. Initially, critics and the public condemned the painting as an incoherent hodgepodge, but the work soon came to be seen as a powerful antiwar statement and remains an iconic symbol of the violence and terror that dominated world events during the remainder of the twentieth century.

The impulse to create art—whether painting animals with crude pigments on a cave wall, sculpting a human form from marble, or commemorating human tragedy in a mural—thus serves many purposes. It offers an entertaining diversion, nourishes the imagination and the spirit, decorates and beautifies the world, and chronicles the age. But underlying all these functions is the desire to reveal that which is obscure—to illuminate, clarify, and perhaps ennoble. As Picasso himself stated, "The purpose of art is washing the dust of daily life off our souls."

The Eye on Art series is intended to assist readers in understanding the various roles of art in society. Each volume offers an in-depth exploration of a major artistic movement, medium, figure, or profession. All books in the series are beautifully illustrated with full-color photographs and diagrams. Riveting narrative, clear technical explanation, informative sidebars, fully documented quotes, a bibliography, and a thorough index all provide excellent starting points for research and discussion. With these features, the Eye on Art series is a useful introduction to the world of art—a world that can offer both insight and inspiration.

 Introduction

The Evolution of Glass

"Throughout history, people have suspected that glass is magic. How else can a material be explained that imitates other materials but cannot itself be imitated? That is five times stronger than steel, yet can be broken by the human voice? That is invoked by heating sand and ash and then bewitched into an infinite variety of forms and textures in an astonishing array of colors? That is hot liquid and frozen solid, transparent and opaque, common and exalted?"

—Karen S. Chambers and Tina Oldknow, *Clearly Inspired: Contemporary Glass and Its Origins*

Glass plays an invaluable role in every aspect of our lives. From the mirrors in which we evaluate ourselves every morning, to the lighting systems at work or in the classroom, to the flat screen television at home, glass is everywhere. It is in architecture, cameras, scientific and medical instruments, household utensils and dishes, automobiles, and advanced fiber-optics communications systems.

Glass has been useful to society, but it has also evolved into what scientist and glass artist Dominick Labino once described as "a medium through which man could express himself artistically by creating objects of rare beauty. . . . Its visual possibilities are unlimited."[1]

The Basic Ingredients

Three main ingredients are necessary to make glass. Silica is needed in the form of quartz, sand, or flint. An alkali is required, like soda (sodium carbonate) or potash, made from the ashes of burning plants or wood, to reduce the melting point of the silica. Lime from limestone stabilizes the mass, allows it to harden, and prevents deterioration.

Early glassmakers experimented with various ingredients and discovered that metal oxides could be added to color the glass. It was found that cobalt produced rich blues, manganese created purples and pinks, and iron and sulfur generated various shades of yellow. According to Labino, "There are at least 35 elements which can be used as coloring agents: some used alone, others in combination."[2]

Exact recipes for glass differed by region and from one glassmaker to another. Ancient Mesopotamian cuneiform tablets

A glass flower sculpture by Dale Chihuly called the *Persian Chandelier*, 2005, hangs from the ceiling of Temperate House at the Royal Botanic Gardens, Kew, in Richmond, Surrey, England.

from 650 B.C. described a two-step process to create glass. First the ingredients were crushed and mixed together, then fired over a low heat. Then the mixture was ground down again and fired a second time over higher heat. The resulting mass cooled into a solid piece of glass. This was broken into chunks and transported to glassmakers throughout the ancient world, where they were remelted and worked into a variety of glassware.

Functional and Decorative

The earliest glass was used in beads to make jewelry or for trading. Glass vessels, containers, and other decorative pieces in the ancient world were only affordable to the wealthy. Most people used pottery for their cups and tableware. After the discovery of glassblowing in Roman times, simple and affordable glassware for the table became available for every family. Glass could be easily washed, and cleaner dishes promoted better health.

Window glass let light into otherwise dark and dusty interiors, lengthening the day. With windows came the ability to let

Modern glassmakers, like the one pictured here, may work alone or with a team, using a variety of techniques and materials.

in more fresh air. "Transparent glass lets in light so house dirt becomes apparent," explained writers Alan MacFarlane and Gerry Martin. "The glass itself must be clean to be effective. So glass, both from its nature and the effects it has, is favorable to hygiene."[3]

As glass formulas and techniques became more sophisticated, mirrors were produced, then lenses and prisms, which led to the development of eyeglasses, magnification, telescopes, and other scientific advancements. Glass greenhouses allowed longer growing seasons for flowers and even fruits and vegetables, which made diets healthier.

Functional glass coexisted with the manufacture of more decorative and ornamental glass pieces. Glass styles developed by geographical region and spread throughout the world. Soon, functional and decorative merged into one, resulting in superbly crafted and beautiful tableware in various styles using the most pure and brilliant lead glass ingredients and advanced cutting and decorative techniques.

Artistic Glass

Increased industrialization combined with new technological advancements resulted in the creation of specialized machines that could rapidly produce glass in great quantities. Reaction to machine-made mass-produced glassware led to the nineteenth-century Art Nouveau and twentieth-century Art Deco styles. Individual glass artists emerged from the factories and became well known for their unique designs. Later, artists working in private studios began to produce original glassworks that were neither functional nor decorative. Some were a statement of form and content, others conveyed the artist's emotions and opinions.

Contemporary glass artists include a wide range of men and women, working alone or with a team, using a diversity of techniques with an extensive variety of materials. Sometimes they employ the latest technology or utilize the simplest of processes. Some even revive ancient glassmaking methods. Though the manner and materials may differ, all have chosen glass as their artistic and expressive medium.

Ancient Origins

"The methods and ingredients used to make glass and the tools used to form it, have probably changed less throughout the centuries than those used in any other art."

—Toledo Museum of Art, *Art in Glass*

Natural glass has always existed on the earth in several forms. A volcanic glass called obsidian is formed when molten rock from a volcano cools too quickly for the minerals to crystallize. Primitive man used obsidian for knives, spears, and other weapons and tools.

Long, thin tubes of glass are sometimes formed after lightning strikes the ground. Other natural glass called tektites are thought to be the result of the impact of meteorites with rocks or formed by fusion as they enter the earth's atmosphere. The first tektites were discovered in the 1930s and consisted mainly of silica (80 percent). Australian tektites were thought to be less than 1 million years old, while those found in North America were 33 million years old.

First Written Account

"Although it would give a kind of satisfaction to be able to say that a certain man invented glass at a certain time and place," wrote historian Mary Luella Trowbridge, "we can only speculate on its origins."[4] Most glass experts agree that glass was first manufactured between 3000 and 2000 B.C. The earliest written account was by Pliny the Elder, Roman author of *Natural History*. Pliny attributed the discovery of glassmaking to Phoenician sea traders who settled on the Syrian coast and sailed throughout the Mediterranean selling and trading goods.

According to Pliny, who died shortly after the eruption of Mount Vesuvius on August 29 in the year A.D. 79, the Phoenicians were preparing for their evening meal on the sandy coast near the mouth of the Belus River. "They spread out along the shore to make a meal. There were no stones to support their cooking-pots, so they placed lumps of soda from their ship under them. When these became hot and fused with the sand on the beach, streams from an unknown translucent liquid flowed and this was the origin of glass."[5]

Many historians discount Pliny's narrative and point to the fact that a campfire would not be hot enough to fuse the sand with the soda. If it did somehow occur, the result would not be

Tektites like the one shown here are created when a large meteor strikes the earth.

Pliny the Elder attributed the discovery of glassmaking to Phoenician sea traders.

glass, but a solution of sodium silicate, which was sometimes called water-glass. What was missing and necessary for glass production was the addition of lime, which Pliny did not mention.

An Accidental Discovery

For hundreds of years, ancient pottery was made from quartz-rich sand combined with soda and other ingredients. Many experts believe that glass was discovered in the course of making such ceramic objects. During firing, the high-heating stage necessary to create this pottery, glass may have inadvertently resulted from a misfiring or related process.

Most experts agree that glass developed from ceramic glazes over a long period of time. Art historian J.R. Vavra declared, "Such raw material when melted in the fire, became unintentionally and accidentally, glass."[6] Labino wrote: "It is possible that a glaze which rolled from an overfired pot and cooled produced glass beads. . . . It could have been in this way that man discovered glass, not just as a material already formed but as a material he could form himself."[7] Writer Frederic Neuburg explained that "a common method of glazing pottery consisted in steeping the vessel in brine and refiring, whereupon a glass film was formed on the vessel by the interaction of the silica contained in the clay and the sodium of the brine."[8]

According to experts from the Toledo Museum of Art, "The shift . . . from ceramics to glass . . . could seem a major technological revolution."[9] The reason for this is that ceramics are formed when the clay is wet and cold. The formation of glass occurs when the material is molten hot, harder to control, and potentially dangerous. The cold ceramic form is brought to a certain temperature in a closed kiln to solidify the finished product. "With glass . . . ," explained the Toledo Museum experts, "a process nearly opposite is required. The raw materials must be withdrawn hot from an open furnace to be formed either with tools or in a mold and then placed in an oven for controlled cooling."[10]

Glass most likely originated either in the Middle East, Egypt, Mesopotamia (now Iraq), or Syria, all of which were major glassmaking centers in the ancient world. These centers depended upon local supplies of sand, soda, and wood for fuel and ashes.

Earliest Evidence of Glass

Glass was first manufactured as a way to reproduce precious stones and their unique colors for personal adornment. Glass beads used as jewelry and glass amulets used as good luck charms have been found that may date back thousands of years. The earliest surviving glass vessels such as cups or bottles date back to the late sixteenth and early fifteenth century B.C. Several glasses bearing the name in hieroglyphics of the Eighteenth

Glass beads such as these were first manufactured as a way to reproduce precious stones such as emeralds and rubies.

Dynasty pharaoh Thutmose III (1490–1437 B.C.) have been found intact.

Glassware of the Eighteenth Dynasty was noted for its bright colors of dark blue, turquoise blue, yellow, and white. This suggests the Egyptians had already perfected techniques of glassmaking or adapted the methods of glassmakers from the Near East. Since the appearance of Egyptian glass vessels and other glass items occurs suddenly rather than gradually, experts believe the latter may be the case. During the reign of Thutmose III, Egyptian armies expanded the empire into Syria and Mesopotamia. The victors took control of the glass centers in those areas, and may have forcibly brought glassmakers back to Egypt.

Major glass objects belonging to other Eighteenth Dynasty pharaohs have also been discovered. The earliest glass sculpture found was a *shawabti*, a mummy figurine that acted as a helper

THE EARLIEST GLASS

Glass beads have played a role not just in art history, but in the world's economic and cultural history. According to writers Karen S. Chambers and Tina Oldknow:

They have served as a medium of exchange for barter and as monetary units in market systems. In America alone, they purchased everything from real estate (Manhattan Island) to human lives (African slaves). Beads have been worn to communicate social status, advertise political alliances, and protect from evil. . . . The "eye" bead is still used throughout the Mediterranean. . . . They are designed to protect the wearer from harmful influences, especially the evil eye.

Karen S. Chambers and Tina Oldknow, *Clearly Inspired: Contemporary Glass and Its Origins.* Maldon, England: Pomegranate, 1999, p. 14.

in the Egyptian afterworld of the dead. The *shawabti* belonged to Ken-Amun, chief steward of Pharaoh Amenhotep II. A portrait sculpture in glass of Amenhotep II was also discovered, as was a glass headrest belonging to Pharaoh Tutankhamen (c. 1346–1337 B.C.). Two solid pieces of turquoise glass in the headrest were joined together by a gold band. The tomb also contained elaborate glass inlays inserted into furniture.

The glass trade in Mesopotamia and Syria developed along with Egypt at this time. All used the same basic methods for creating glass—core forming, molded or cast glass, and mosaic glass, although some pieces were carved from solid blocks, such as the Tutankhamen headrest.

Ancient Methods of Creating Glass

Core forming was a method of winding molten glass around a clay core that was attached to a metal, iron, or wooden rod. The purpose of the core was to shape the vessel. After a controlled cooling (annealing) to relieve stress in the glass, the core was then removed. The core material may have been a mixture of sand or clay and organic material like animal waste, grass, or decomposing vegetation.

The core had to be solid enough to withstand the molten glass, yet soft enough to be dug out when the vessel cooled. The core was shaped by hand with water and then attached to the rod. Next it was dried thoroughly and then fired.

Several techniques for applying glass around the core were used at one time or another. The core was coated with crushed glass, and then the glass was melted around it. The core was dipped directly into a pot of molten glass. The glass was poured onto the core in thin threads as it was rotated, until it was completely covered. In this technique, the glass was usually applied from top to bottom, and a flat tool or metal rod was used to roll and smooth the threads on a slab of stone (marver). This process was often repeated to build up layers of glass into the desired shape. Decorative colored threads were then applied, using the same rotating technique.

Handles, a foot or base, or a special neck could be added by repeatedly reheating the vessel. The finished piece was cooled slowly, the rod was removed, and the core was picked out. Glass vessels were routinely made using the core-forming method until the invention of glassblowing.

Molded (Cast) and Mosaic Glass

Molding or casting glass, also referred to as slump casting, was first used to make beads and small ornaments. Molds of sand or clay were made into the desired shape and filled with crushed glass. These open, uncovered molds were then heated to melt the glass, which softened and conformed to the shape of the mold.

Later the Egyptians used closed, covered molds to create different types of vessels and larger objects. Molten glass was poured directly into the mold through a small hole. After annealing, the surface of the vessel was finished by using a fast-turning rotating wheel embedded with an abrasive powder to grind and polish any imperfections.

As ancient glassmakers perfected their methods of creating glass vessels, they discovered new techniques for decorating them. Applied thread decoration was one of the most common patterns. Spiral threads of glass were dragged upward or downward to create feather patterns. Other threads were applied vertically to appear as a series of hanging loops or chains, called festoon patterns. Threads of different colors were often twisted together and applied to the neck or rim of a vessel. Sometimes, raised petals or fins were worked into the glass, or the glass was drawn out into thornlike protrusions called prunts.

After annealing, pointed tools were used to make lines or marks on the glass. Rotating wheels of stone or iron enabled the artist to cut simple lines, round grooves, or smooth flat facets on the surface of the glass (as in gemstones).

The technique of making mosaic glass developed in Mesopotamia by 1500 to 1000 B.C. and spread to Egypt. Mosaic glass was made from multicolored rods of glass called canes. Writer Chloe Zerwick described the process:

Egyptologist W.M. Flinders Petrie described a glassmaking house he discovered from the time of Pharaoh Amenhotep IV in fourteenth-century-B.C. Egypt:

> The glass used by the Egyptians at that time was pure; that is not colorless but of a shade that could be given a great variety of hues. It . . . consisted of pure quartzite, ground flints and alkali derived from woodash. This mixture was melted in clay pots, in earlier periods apparently in pits, later in furnaces. Non-transparent colours were added which were thoroughly known already to glassmakers at that time.

> According to historian J.R. Vavra, an analysis of old Egyptian glass showed that it contained about 60 percent quartz sand, 6 percent lime, 20 percent soda, and around 4 percent potash, in addition to small amounts of manganese, oxides of lead, tin, copper, iron, aluminum, and sulfur for coloring.

These Egyptian glass vessels were used to hold cosmetics.

Quoted in J.R. Vavra, *5,000 Years of Glassmaking.* Prague, Czechoslovakia: Artia, 1954, p. 18.

The rods were bundled together to form a design, visible in cross sections. The bundle was fused [melted together] and the resulting large rod was heated and pulled out like taffy. The design remained the same, except that it got smaller and smaller as the rod became longer and longer. The rod was then cut into slices, each having the same identical design, which could be arranged in various patterns.[11]

Apis Worship

A famous Egyptian mosaic is of the sacred black bull Apis, which was the animal form of the god Osiris. According to glass historian Robert Charleston, "The center of Apis worship was at Memphis [a major ancient Egyptian city], where solemn rites of great complexity were enacted whenever the bull of the moment died."[12] The dead bull was embalmed and then taken to a special gravesite, which was very difficult considering the weight of the corpse. Then a search began for the new Apis bull, which had to be a solid black animal with a white triangular blaze on its head. The Apis mosaic reveals the symbol of a cobra poised ready to strike on a sun disk between the horns. The small, decorative plaque was probably used as an inlay, inserted into the surface of a wall or piece of furniture.

"A Commodity of High Luxury"

According to historians at the Toledo Museum of Art, "Ancient glass was a commodity of high luxury and . . . was owned by only the very wealthy."[13] Zerwick declared, "In Egypt, no one but pharaohs, high priests, and nobles owned glass."[14] While most people used ceramic cups and containers, the richest members of society owned glass, which was valued highly along with gold, silver, ivory and other precious gems. Only the upper classes owned glass containers, bottles, and flasks that held perfumes and valuable medicinal ointments. Some used glass to decorate archways, ceilings, walls, and furniture.

de la carte et kildy graces a nixf: de somuciur que dieu
luy auoit faicte qui estoit sains sauf descendu a terre

Come alixandre se fist aualer en vint toneau de verr
woe les elusoes della duter de lumiers ...

According to legend, Alexander the Great explored the sea in a glass diving jar.

King Solomon in the tenth century B.C. supposedly paved his palace floors with glass. An Arabian legend relates that the Queen of Sheba mistakenly thought there was water in King Solomon's palace because the glass floors gleamed so brightly. Another legend related by Zerwick involved Alexander the Great, the third-century-B.C. conqueror, who was reputed to have "descended into the sea in a huge glass jar to observe the plants and fishes there."[15] Drawings of this event show Alexander in his fancy robes beneath the ocean in a large, transparent glass ball, held up by members of the royal court.

Although they did not own it or use it very often, the lower classes did have a connection to glass. According to Trowbridge, "The poor people seem to have gone to the glass-factories to get warm."[16] Trowbridge wrote that glass-factories were "lounging places for the poor."[17]

BEFORE MAKING GLASS, FOLLOW THESE DIRECTIONS

In the ancient world, glassmaking was a mystical and spiritual undertaking that required certain preliminary steps. The following Mesopotamian cuneiform text was excavated at the Library of Ashurbanipal, in the ancient city of Nineveh.

When you set up a kiln to make glass, first search for a favorable month and a propitious day. . . . As soon as you have completely finished building the kiln, go and place Kuba-images there. . . . On the day you plan to place the [glass] in the kiln, make a sheep sacrifice before the Kuba-images, place juniper incense on the censer, pour out a libation of honey and liquid butter, and only then make a fire in the hearth of the kiln and place the [glass] inside.

Quoted in Karen S. Chambers and Tina Oldknow, *Clearly Inspired: Contemporary Glass and Its Origins.* Maldon, England: Pomegranate, 1999, p. 14.

All Roads Lead to Rome

The basic techniques of glassmaking in the ancient world were improved and refined through the centuries, even as Rome expanded from a small republic into a vast and powerful empire. At its height, the Roman Empire included much of Europe and the Middle East and absorbed the major glassmaking centers in Mesopotamia, Egypt, and Syria.

A landmark event occurred during this period of Roman domination that radically changed the future of glass. The discovery of glassblowing took place sometime in the middle of the first century B.C., along the same Phoenician coast where Pliny wrote that glass originated.

Roman Glass and the Discovery of Glassblowing

Most experts agree that glassmaking history was completely revolutionized by the realization that glass could be formed and shaped by blowing. It is believed that glassblowing began around 50 B.C. somewhere along the Syrian coast. The subsequent increase in glass production coincided with the rise of the Roman Empire (30 B.C.–A.D. 476).

Writer C.J. Phillips wrote: "The invention of the blowpipe, even though time and place cannot be fixed with certainty, must be considered one of the truly great discoveries of mankind. It caused an industrial revolution which changed glass from a luxury into a necessity. It . . . made possible the quantity production of glass articles in shapes and designs previously impossible to produce."[18]

Free Blowing and Mold Blowing

"A now nameless—probably Syrian—glassworker realized, perhaps through an accident with the nozzle of a furnace bellows," states a Toledo Museum of Art publication, "that glass could be gathered on the end of a metal pipe and formed by inflation."[19] In this technique, called free blowing, the glassmaker used a long iron or clay tube called a blowpipe, which was dipped into molten glass. A gob of the glass (called a gather or parison) was picked up with one end of the blowpipe. Then the glassmaker blew into the tube, inflated a bubble of glass, and rotated and worked it with pincers and other tools into many different shapes and sizes.

In mold blowing, the parison was blown out into a reusable open or closed mold, which had a specific shape, geometric pattern, or scene. In this way, the glass could be created quickly in

ENNION OF SIDON

Some of the best glassblowers were from Sidon on the Syrian coast. The Romans thought so highly of these Syrian glassmakers that they were given the honorable title of Roman citizen. Among the Sidonians, the most popular and well known was Ennion, whose signed works are exhibited in museums around the world today.

Ennion was one of the earliest glassmakers to use the technique of mold blowing. He seemed to dislike repetition and often changed the colors and features of his mold-blown vessels. A series of fifteen handled cups with Ennion's signature have been found in northern Italy, suggesting that Ennion either moved from Sidon or opened a branch of his glass factory there. He signed his work in Greek with the phrase, "Ennion made [me]." Some of his vessels are signed with the words, "Let the buyer remember [me],"[1] apparently in hopes of future sales.

A signed Ennion cup was found at Corinth in Greece along with a coin dated about A.D. 40. Historians believe that this helps to date part of Ennion's early career. According to glass expert Robert Charleston, "The Ennion glasses are the most elegant of all the mold-blown glasses—with

clear and well-drawn ornaments sharply reproduced in the new technique."[2]

This glass jar is signed by Ennion of Sidon, one of the earliest glassmakers to use the technique of mold blowing.

1. Quoted in Robert J. Charleston, *Masterpieces of Glass: A World History from the Corning Museum of Glass.* New York: Abrams, 1990, p. 43.

2. Charleston, *Masterpieces of Glass*, p. 43.

one step, over and over again. If further decorations were desired, the glass was removed from the mold, and then handles, rims, stems, or other embellishments were added.

Glassblowing required much higher temperatures than previous glassmaking methods. Open hearths and small kilns evolved into larger, closed furnaces capable of creating molten glass. Glassblowing simplified the process of producing a variety of vessels in a shorter period of time. The industry quickly expanded into the mass production of simple and inexpensive glassware. Glass dishes, jugs, vases, beakers, pitchers, and other containers became common household items throughout the Roman Empire.

The Roman Empire and the Spread of Glass

About the time that glassblowing was discovered, the Roman Empire slowly expanded through military conquest to include countries such as Spain, Britain, Gaul, Macedonia, Greece, Egypt, Palestine, and Syria. Rome was a bustling center of commerce, the arts, and culture for centuries. At its height, the city had a population of a million people, a police force, aqueducts which provided water, excellent sanitation, theaters, firefighters, and even a welfare program for the poor.

Rome was the crossroads of the world, and glass quickly became a valuable trading commodity. The unified and stable empire provided a framework for widespread trade routes and exchanges with other cultures. Just as glass products traveled everywhere, so did the glassmakers. The techniques of glassblowing, which started in the Middle East, spread throughout the lands controlled by Rome. Glass factories were started in Cologne, Germany, and throughout Italy, as well as other areas. Roman glass has even been found in China and Japan, presumably shipped there along eastern trade routes.

Glass containers of various styles and sizes were used to transport liquids, perfumes, wines, and other items of commerce throughout the empire. Such containers were also used to conserve and store food, drink, medicines, and toiletries. Glass was

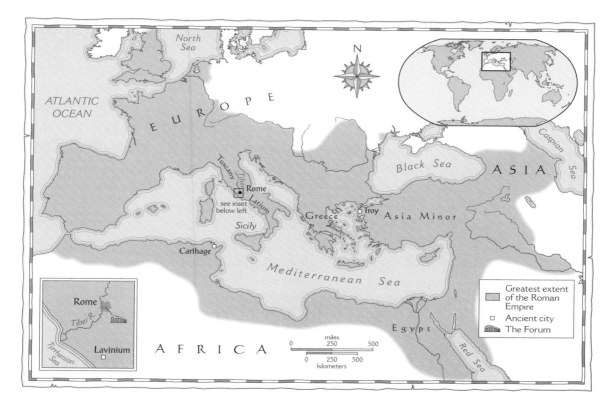

A map of the Roman Empire at its height. At the same time that glassblowing was discovered, the Roman Empire was expanding.

sanitary, nonporous, and odorless, making it ideal for preservation and the prevention of disease. The containers were often packed in straw for land or sea travel and were reusable after cleaning. According to Robert Charleston: "Plain bottles of considerable size, square for ease of packing, were used for the transport of oil. . . . Only their flattened handles were decorated, by means of vertical ribbing, which earns them the name of 'celery handles.'"[20]

Alan MacFarlane and Gerry Martin declared that "the Romans have a central place in the history of glass. They provided not only the technical skills but a sense of glass as an important material in its own right."[21]

Glass for Every Occasion

Glassmakers began to experiment with mold-blown whimsical shapes and produced large quantities of vessels shaped like animals, human heads, or clusters of grapes and other fruit. During

Roman chariot races or gladiatorial contests, glassmakers sold souvenir glass beakers with scenes of their favorite fighter or charioteer. Drinking vessels were often inscribed with greetings such as "Rejoice and be merry,"[22] or "Take the victory."[23]

Tina Oldknow wrote: "Thousands of preserved blown-glass flasks, bottles, plates, vials, bowls, cups, and jars testify to the immediate popularity of glassblowing in the Roman world. Easy to clean, dispose of, and replace, versatile, watertight, attractive, and colorful, glass was a highly functional material that literally changed the way people lived."[24]

Glass was so widespread throughout the empire that it became cheaper and easier just to throw away damaged pieces and buy a replacement. "A glass bowl or drinking cup may be purchased for a copper coin,"[25] wrote the Greek historian Strabo around 19 A.D.

Clear Glass

Among the upper classes, the favorite drink in the Roman Empire was wine, the color of which ranged from a deep red to light rose to white. Clearer glass helped intensify the appreciation and appeal of the wine. The demand for colorless glass grew, so manganese oxide was added to finer, more expensive vessels to eliminate any hints of color. The clearer the glass, the

more desired it became. "The most highly prized glass is transparent," wrote Pliny the Elder, "and its appearance is as close as possible to that of rock-crystal."[26]

The preference for looking through glass at what was inside had future implications in glass development. "The long-term consequence of clear glass manufacture was the development of glass as a thinking tool, through mirrors, lenses, and spectacles,"[27] wrote MacFarlane and Martin.

Upper-class Romans preferred clear glass vessels that allowed them to enjoy the color of wine.

Cameo Glass

The mass production of utilitarian glassware was accompanied by elaborate glassmaking techniques to make special decorative items for the very rich, which remain unique to this day. When making cameo glass, a still-hot blown vessel of background glass, which was usually a dark blue color, was either dipped into a pot of a contrasting color like opaque white or blown into a

The Portland vase is the most famous example of Roman cameo glass.

preformed bowl or cup of a contrasting color. It was a vessel of one color covered by another layer of glass of a different color. Sometimes this procedure was repeated with additional layers.

The carvers then completed the cameo glass process by cutting figures and designs in the outer white layer to reveal the colored background layer underneath. "The true refinement of the art," explained Charleston, "was to cut the opaque white layer so thin in places that the blue ground partially showed through, producing tonal as well as purely sculptural effects."[28]

Roman cameo glass is one of the rarest types of blown glass. There are little more than a dozen complete pieces in existence today, and about two hundred fragments of vessels. A fragment of a six-layer cameo glass cup is exhibited at the Corning Museum of Glass in Corning, New York. The cut is so thin and delicate that each layer is exposed, resulting in a subtle variation of shade and color. The most famous example of cameo glass is the Portland vase exhibited in the British Museum in London. The name comes from the Duchess of Portland, one of several owners of the vase, which was discovered in sixteenth-century Rome in the tomb of Roman emperor Severus Alexander, who died in A.D. 235.

Historian Robin Brooks described the Portland vase in great detail:

A decorative frieze runs around the body of the vase where an outer skin of white glass has been carved away, leaving figures in relief, against the deep blue backdrop to the scene. The carving is extraordinarily delicate. . . . Two handles of blue glass connect the neck with the shoulder of the vase. Below these runs the frieze of figures set in a landscape of stylized trees and rocks. There are seven figures, divided into two scenes by the handles.[29]

Experts differ as to the identity of the figures on the vase. At one time or another, they were believed to be Neptune, Helen of Troy, Achilles, Venus, Augustus Caesar, and even Cleopatra and Marc Antony.

Extraordinary and Elaborate

Roman cage cups, also called *diatreta*, are glass vessels that are completely encircled by an open enclosure of glass that is attached to the main vessel by several supporting braces or struts. These cups are very rare, and experts consider them among the most complicated ever made in the ancient world. According to Oldknow, the cage cup "represents one of the most elusive and sophisticated of the ancient luxury techniques for glass. Although many attempts . . . have been made to reproduce the cage cups during the twentieth century, it

Roman cage cups, also called *diatreta*, are very rare and are considered the most complicated vessels ever made in the ancient world.

still is not known precisely how ancient Roman glassmakers or engravers made them."[30]

"Using wheels fed with an abrasive paste," explained Chloe Zerwick, "the cutter removed most of the glass from a thick walled 'blank,' leaving a cup or bowl-shaped vessel imprisoned in a fragile openwork 'cage.'"[31] The ornamental outside network around the vessel stood completely free of the inside surface except for the few supports. The most famous example of *diatreta* is the Lycurgus cup at the British Museum in London.

POPULONIA BOTTLES

Several of a series of souvenir flasks were found at Populonia, near Florence, Italy, in the nineteenth century. These greenish bottles were characterized by a light, shallow type of engraving in which the surface of the vessel was slightly touched with the edge of a rotating wheel. The bottles illustrate different landscape scenes and public buildings of the ancient seaside resorts of Puteoli and Baiae. Some of the vessels were inscribed with the names of wealthy guests who took them home as souvenirs from their vacation at the shore.

The engraving on a bottle exhibited at the Corning Museum of Glass sounds like a newspaper advertisement. As translated, it reads, "Long life to you, happy soul," and "The pool. The palace. The oyster-beds. The shore." The pool apparently refers to an artificial lake built by Emperor Nero. According to Roman historian Suetonius, "Nero . . . undertook to build a pool . . . covered by a roof and enclosed by porticoes, into which he intended to turn all the hot springs which existed through the whole of Baiae." One Populonia bottle was part of the art collection of Elise Bonaparte, Napoléon's sister. Others have been found in Portugal and Poland.

Quoted in Robert J. Charleston, *Masterpieces of Glass: A World History from the Corning Museum of Glass*. New York: Abrams, 1990, p. 55.

Other Roman Glassmaking Techniques

Millefiori, which means a thousand flowers in Italian, is a technique closely related to fused mosaic glass in which the resulting pattern resembles many small blossoms. Decorative glass canes, or rods, were sliced and embedded in clear glass. Frederic Neuburg explained the process:

> The true millefiori . . . glass was produced when rods of one color were given one or more casings [layers] of different colored glass. . . . If instead of a rod a glass tube was cased several times . . . the result was a flower. The multi-colored flowers of varying size and shape produced in this way . . . [resulted in a] . . . bowl resembling a bed of flowers of singular brilliance.[32]

Large and small ribbed glass bowls were mass produced in Rome mainly in blue and green colors. They were characterized by a number of narrow to thick ribs that started at the rim of the vessel and met at the base. The number of ribs ranged from about six or seven to more than thirty.

Most experts agree that the bowls were made with ribbed molds, while some believe they were made with a rib stamp pressed onto the soft glass or the use of a lathe. "It seems evident they were made in ribbed molds," asserted Charleston. "Whether this was achieved by pressing or by slow melting of glass in the form of powder or small fragments, it is not clear, partly because the traces of how the bowls were made have been removed by subsequent grinding and polishing on the wheel."[33]

Decorations for Glass

Snake-thread glass most likely originated in Syria and was improved and cultivated in Cologne in the Rhineland in the second to third century A.D. Curved and winding ribbon designs of trailing threads were applied separately to the surface of blown glass with a flame. The ribbons were smoothed on the outside of the vessel with the use of a saw-edged tool that left slanted lines.

Syrian snake-thread glass was characterized by trailing threads of a single color, whereas a variety of colored ribbons were used in Cologne.

Another form of decoration was dappled glass, in which chips or kernels of multicolored glass were loosely spread on the surface of a vessel before it was fully blown. These fused with the glass and thinned out with additional blowing to form colorful splashes of color. Sometimes the chips or kernels were applied to a hot surface after the glass was blown, and they stood out as a relief decoration. Glass objects were also adorned with gold banding or gold leaf. Luxurious glass boxes decorated with gold bands were made for the very rich to store ointments and creams. Bands of multicolored glass were carefully fused together with layers of gold leaf in these handmade vessels.

In Roman times, glass was sometimes engraved with decorative patterns. Engraving was done with a hard-point tool or a rotating round, flat, or beveled (slanted) wheel with abrasive powder, which cut lightly, deeply, or jagged and rough. Another form of decoration, called enameling, was used. Enameling is a type of painting in which ground-up colored glass was mixed with oil until it resembled paint. It was then applied to the surface of the glass and heated so the enamel fused with the glass. Another type of painting, called reverse painting, was applied to clear, cold glass (which was not fired) and allowed the drinker to view a scene painted on the back of the vessel.

Decorating with Glass

Home interiors of wealthy Romans contained inlaid glass on walls, ceilings, furniture, and lamps. The Roman philosopher Seneca declared, "A person finds himself poor and base unless his vaulted ceiling is covered with glass."[34] Pliny wrote that

> Scaurus built the greatest building ever constructed by man. . . . This was a theatre that had a three-tiered stage with 360 columns. . . . The lowest tier of the stage was of marble, the middle one of glass—an unheard of example of extravagance even in later times—and the

top one of gilded planks. The columns of the lowest tier were each almost 38 feet high. . . . The auditorium held 80,000.[35]

Decline and Fall of the Roman Empire

With the decline of the Roman Empire and the fall of Rome in A.D. 476, "lavishly decorated bowls . . . [and other glassware] . . .

FUN AND GAMES

The use of glass in the Roman Empire was not just about function or luxury. They also had fun with it. According to glass historian Mary Luella Trowbridge:

> The Romans had a game . . . which somewhat resembled modern checkers. . . . The pawns, which seem frequently to have been made of glass were called . . . soldier, enemy, and mercenary or robber. . . . It must have been a kind of "catch the robbers" game, like "fox and geese," only on a board . . . black and white pawns were used . . . gaming boards were also inlaid with glass.

> Some Roman glassmakers were practical jokers. They built an inverted bottle in the form of a glass, in which the bottom portion was pushed up to form a double wall. When the glass was filled up through the neck then closed and turned over, the liquid flowed between the walls. The glass appeared full, but nothing would come out, frustrating many thirsty Romans.

Mary Luella Trowbridge, *Philological Studies in Ancient Glass*. Urbana: University of Illinois Press, 1930, p. 183.

A story has been passed down by ancient historians Suetonius, Pliny the Elder, and Isidore of Seville about a glassmaker who invented a flexible, unbreakable glass during the reign of the Roman emperor Tiberius (14–37 A.D.). Supposedly, the glass was thrown to the floor. It did not break, but became dented, and the glassmaker easily repaired the dent with his hammer.

The emperor was very impressed by the display and asked the man if he had told anyone about his secret. When the glassmaker assured Tiberius that no one else knew of the existence of the unbreakable glass, the emperor promptly had him beheaded and his workshop completely demolished. Tiberius feared that if the secret of this glass became public, it would destroy the value of gold and other metals like copper and silver.

Some glass experts believe that the patterned surfaces of mold-blown glass may have been confused with the hammered surfaces of metal objects, thus inspiring this Roman legend. Others believe it was just a tall tale.

Roman emperor Tiberius is said to have destroyed the secret of unbreakable glass.

were no longer in demand," declared historian Charleen K. Edwards. "Factories closed when markets diminished as a result of political unrest and frequent invasions."[36]

Though glass output decreased and techniques became simpler and less elegant, glass production continued at the fringes of the former empire. The Germanic Franks produced cone beakers that were characterized by having no base or foot. Since they could not be put down, these drinking glasses were continuously refilled. The Franks developed a new technique to decorate the body of other drinking vessels. They blew the glass outward into thin, hollow projections, referred to as claws, which curved downward and attached to the foot of the vessel.

The Middle Ages (fifth to fifteenth century A.D.) followed the collapse of the Roman Empire. The growing power of the Christian Church stimulated glassmaking for church rituals, and glass production also flourished in the Islamic Middle East and Persia. Gradually, Italian glassmaking revived, and by the Renaissance, the Venetians dominated the world of glass.

3 The Spread of Glassmaking: Middle Eastern and Venetian Glass

"God (Allah) is the light of the Heavens and the Earth. His light is as a niche in which a lamp, the lamp in a glass, the glass as it were a glittering star."

—Passage from the Koran, quoted in Robert J. Charleston, *Masterpieces of Glass: A World History from the Corning Museum of Glass*

"During the Renaissance and for centuries beyond, Venetian glass-blowers became so technically proficient and important to the history of the medium that even today Venice is considered the spiritual center of glassmaking, the historic home of a craft that is nearly six thousand years old."

—Karen S. Chambers and Tina Oldknow, *Clearly Inspired: Contemporary Glass and Its Origins*

In the sixth century, the glass industry continued to develop and thrive in eastern areas such as Persia, Syria, Macedonia, and Asia Minor (what is now Turkey), despite the fall of Rome and the decrease of glass production in western areas such as northern Italy and parts of Europe. The Roman Empire no longer existed, but Roman glassmaking techniques and design continued to influence the production of glass in other existing and successive cultures. Sasanian Persia, the Islamic empire, the Byzantine Empire, and later the Venetian glass industry elaborated on Roman methods to create new, individual characteristics of style, shape, and form.

Sasanian Persia

The Sasanian dynasty controlled Persia (what is now Iran) from about the third to the seventh century A.D. "They were a cultivated, powerful people . . . ," wrote Chloe Zerwick, "and their glassmakers developed a style of their own . . . distinguished by skillful carving in high relief and the use of applied trail decoration."[37] This glass was usually pale green or transparent in color and thick walled.

Sasanian glassmakers preferred to decorate vessels with deep, wheel-cut facets (many small, polished, flat surfaces as in a cut diamond or other gemstones). These wheel-cut facets varied in

Sasanian glassmakers decorated pieces like this bowl with wheel-cut facets.

depth and were arranged in an overall pattern. Glass cutters often used circular, disk-type patterns and bosses, which were round, knoblike projections. On some particularly thick-walled vessels, the glass between bosses was cut back enough so that the knobs stood raised up in high relief, which required an extensive amount of time and effort. "The luxury glassware made in complicated processes in the Sasanian centers of power," stated art historian Helmut Ricke, ". . . is amongst the greatest achievements in glass history."[38]

The capital of Ctesiphon, located on the Tigris River below Baghdad, was the glassmaking center of Sasanian Persia. Trade was extensive in the empire, and glass was a valuable commodity. Sasanian vases and bowls were distributed widely throughout the area, and some vessels have been found as far away as Japan, Russia, and Copenhagen.

The Sasanian Persian empire was conquered by the Arabs in the seventh century A.D. and became a part of the vast Islamic empire.

Islamic Glass

The followers of the Prophet Muhammad, the founder of Islam who died in A.D. 632, had conquered a vast area that absorbed the Persians and extended from parts of India and China in the east to Sicily, Spain, and Portugal in the west. "In a sense," wrote experts at the Toledo Museum of Art, "Islam had replaced the Roman Empire as the unifying force in the Mediterranean and near Eastern civilization. Because of their rapid expansion into already long civilized areas, the nomadic early Moslems readily assimilated the arts and comforts of the . . . peoples they conquered and converted."[39]

Many Islamic glass vessels had pear-shaped bodies, small spouts, and long, narrow necks, which kept the liquids inside from evaporating too quickly. Although actual images of living people or animals were forbidden to be reproduced by the Islamic religion, glassmakers often did so in an abstract and stylized way. Sprinklers, vessels used for pouring drops of perfume or other liquid, were molded into bird shapes with embedded

HEDWIG GLASSES

Hedwig drinking glasses originated in the Islamic Near East but were named after a European Christian saint, who was said to have used a similar style glass. The Hedwig glasses were characterized by a smoky brown or greenish color, a wide-mouthed beaker shape, and distinctive deep-relief cutting.

According to legend, Saint Hedwig, who died in A.D. 1243, drank only water as part of a religious self-denial ritual. Her husband feared for her health and picked up the beaker that had been filled with water and drank from it. He discovered the water had been changed to wine. After this miracle and the canonization of Saint Hedwig, these glasses were treated as holy relics by the church and brought to the West by the Crusaders.

Only fourteen to twenty Hedwig glasses exist today. The main decorative theme involved running animals. Glass expert Robert Charleston described them "with hatched manes on necks, leaf-shaped feet, and tufted tails, the eye always rendered as a dot in relief and the joint of the thigh often emphasized by a scroll."

Robert J. Charleston, *Masterpieces of Glass: A World History from the Corning Museum of Glass.* New York: Abrams, 1990, p. 75.

threads of glass that represented feathers. Certain types of bottles, called dromedary flasks, were shaped like camels carrying vases on their backs. Many Islamic glassmakers used repeating patterns of plants, angular point and line designs, or inscriptions from the Koran, the Islamic holy book, to decorate glassware.

Roman cameo glass was revived by the Islamic glass industry in the ninth and tenth century A.D. Whereas the Romans used white glass against a dark background, Islamic glassmakers used colored glass on a colorless background. The Corning ewer, a pitcher with a wide spout exhibited at the Corning Museum of Glass, is an example of Islamic cameo glass. The ewer was made of colorless glass that had been dipped in molten green glass. A large portion of the overlay was stripped away, "leaving the green decoration standing in relief on a colorless background,"[40] explained Robert Charleston.

An important new technique called luster painting is believed to have been discovered in Egypt sometime during the seventh to eighth century A.D. A glossy stain made with sulfide of silver was painted onto the surface of the glass vessel. When refired in the furnace, the stain produced colors in the glass that ranged from clear amber to yellow to brown. This method was used on stained-glass windows in the Middle Ages and is still in use today.

Exquisite Craftsmanship

During the twelfth through the fourteenth century A.D., the Syrian city of Damascus became the glassmaking center of the Islamic empire. The city was divided into different sections depending upon the particular craft, and glassmaking was one of many. There was also a requirement that a son must follow in his father's profession to ensure continuity in the craft. The glassware created in Damascus was of the highest quality.

Many art experts agree that the greatest contribution of Islamic glassmaking was the production of enameled and gilded glass. Enameling was a process in which powdered glasses of various colors were mixed with oil of lavender to form a paste, then painted on the surface of a vessel and heated in an oven to attach the design permanently to the glass. Similarly, gilded painting consisted of finely ground gold powder mixed with oil until it was able to be brushed onto the glass surface and then fired.

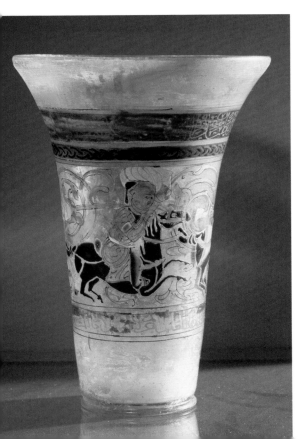

This blown-glass goblet with enamel and gilding dates to thirteenth-century Syria. Enameled and gilded glass was the greatest contribution of Islamic glassmakers.

In 1400, the city of Damascus fell to Mongol invaders. The glasshouses were destroyed, and the victorious conqueror Tamerlane (also known as Timur the Great) captured the glassmakers and carried them off to the Mongol capital city of Samarqand. This invasion brought an end to Islamic glass production.

The Byzantine Empire

Roman emperor Constantine I rebuilt the ancient city of Byzantium, named it Constantinople, and made it the capital of the Roman Empire in A.D. 330. In 337, Emperor Constantine awarded privileged status to glassmakers and glass cutters and excused them from public office. By 437, the glassworkers were exempted from personal taxation, as were other artists and craftspeople.

During the Byzantine Empire, the Church encouraged the production of glass mosaics with religious imagery like the one pictured here.

After Rome and the western portion of the empire were sacked by invaders, the eastern portion continued to flourish in Greece, Thrace, Macedonia, and Asia Minor. It became known as the Byzantine Empire, blending a Roman-style government with Greek culture and Christianity. Glassmaking centers were located in Constantinople and Corinth in Greece, but few actual examples of Byzantine glass have been found. "Christian burial custom discouraged interment of grave gifts with the deceased," explained Karen S. Chambers and Tina Oldknow. "As a result, we lack as complete a picture of the quantity, available forms and colors of Byzantine and Western medieval glass."[41]

The Church encouraged the production of Byzantine glass mosaics and the manufacture of glass vessels for use in religious services. Gold was often used as decoration, and many mosaics had a gold background. "Gloriously colored religious mosaics

adorned churches," wrote Zerwick. "They were composed of colored glass cast as thin, flat cakes and cut into small pieces . . . made to form rich, golden representations of episodes from the Old and New Testaments."[42]

Constantinople fell to the Ottoman Turkish invaders in 1453, which brought an end to the Byzantine Empire. Glassmakers and other craftspeople probably fled to Venice and other parts of northern Italy and Europe, just as they had after the fall of Damascus in 1400. Meanwhile in Italy, the Venetian Republic and its growing glass industry flourished.

Crossroads of the World

The city of Venice in northeast Italy, by virtue of its sea power and location on the Adriatic Sea, became a city-state, also called a republic. It was also a major center of commerce on the east-west trade route between Europe and Asia. The glass industry in Venice grew steadily from the seventh century, when the first glasshouse was built on the island of Torcello in the Lagoon of Venice. The glass trade became very lucrative and an important part of the economy of the republic.

A glassmaker's guild was formed in the early part of the thirteenth century, and in 1271, the Venetian republic passed an ordinance that banned imports of foreign glass, as well as foreign glassmakers who wished to work in Venice. According to Charleen K. Edwards: "The growing number of glasshouses and the danger of fire led to an edict in 1291 transferring all glassmaking operations to the neighboring island of Murano. There large-scale production could be encouraged without endangering the city, and new techniques and formulas could be developed in relative secrecy."[43]

The Venetian republic wanted to protect its economic monopoly and maintain control over glass secrets such as formulas, techniques, and firing. A law was passed that forbade the glassmakers of Murano from leaving the island upon sentence of death. Despite this restriction, they were very highly regarded in the Venetian community. Zerwick wrote, "Many were given

A map of Murano in Venice. By law, Murano glassmakers were forbidden from leaving the island.

The production and sale of mosque lamps played a significant role in the Islamic economy and were very profitable for glassmakers, some of whom specialized in these items. The Muslim places of holy worship not only used the lamps for light and decoration, but, according to writer Chloe Zerwick, they "were symbolic of the light of God as well."[1] Many were inscribed in enamel with verses from the Koran.

The mosque lamps usually contained a holder for a bowl of oil and a wick, although some had a tube insert in which a candle could be attached. They were suspended from ceilings or walls by three or six chain loops.

A transparent light-amber mosque lamp with enameled and gilded painting is exhibited at the Toledo Museum of Art. The inscription on the lamp, which most likely was a gift to a mosque from a wealthy supporter, read, "By order of His Excellency, the Noblest, the High, the Liegeman, the Master, as-Saifi, Sheikhu the Victorious."[2]

Mosque lamps like the one seen here were an important part of the Islamic economy.

1. Chloe Zerwick, *A Short History of Glass.* New York: Abrams, 1990, p. 45.

2. Quoted in Toledo Museum of Art, *Art in Glass.* Toledo, Ohio: Toledo Museum of Art, 1969, p. 41.

patrician standing, their daughters being permitted to marry noblemen."[44]

The Glass Itself

A glassmaker named Angelo Barovier (about 1400 to 1460) was the inventor of *cristallo*, the thin, colorless, ductile, elegant, light glass that made the Venetian industry famous. It imitated rock crystal, which was very expensive and thought to contain magical qualities.

Cristallo was created by using the very purest of materials. Art historian David Whitehouse described the process: "Cristallo was developed by carefully selecting quartzite pebbles from the Ticino River (to provide an unusually pure form of silica) and plant ash from the Levant (to provide the alkali that reduced the temperature at which the silica melted)." The resultant glass "remained soft and workable for longer than most other glass mixtures," which allowed it to be "transformed into objects of breathtaking grace and fragility."[45]

Cristallo "became so popular that trips to glasshouses to observe Muranese glassblowers at work became one of the favorite attractions Venice offered its important visitors,"[46] wrote Chambers and Oldknow. Alan MacFarlane and Gerry Martin declared, "Its purity and thinness was an object of fascination and desire."[47]

The foreign markets were inundated with *cristallo* glassware. Venetian glassmakers even filled special orders for customers from other countries. A seventeenth-century English tourist wrote: "Another day we went to Murano again to see the glasshouses which furnish almost all Europe with drinking glasses. They utter here forth two hundred thousand crowns worth a year of this brittle wares; and they seem to have taken measure of every nations belly and humour, to fit them with drinking glasses accordingly."[48]

Enameling and Gilding

In the fifteenth century, Venetian glass, influenced by Islamic wares, also included very ornate, heavily enameled, and gilded

Fifteenth-century Venetian glass, like this enameled chalice, was influenced by Islamic glass decorating

vessels. Classical scenes, intricate floral patterns, coats of arms, and portraits were painted on glass surfaces that ranged in color from clear and opaque white to blue, green, and red. "Decorating a glass . . . was a lengthy matter," explained Charleston. "The gold was applied in leaf form as the last process of marking the glass itself and was welded to the surface in the heat of the furnace. The glass was then annealed and sent to the decorator's studio . . . where it was painted with enamels."[49]

Although enameled and gilded decoration declined in Venetian glass in the sixteenth century, diamond-point engraving was widely used for simple but elegant floral designs and delicate line decorations. According to Ricke, "With a diamond point set into a holder, the decorator scratches ornamentation, writing, or figural depictions into the glass surface."[50]

The malleable characteristic of *cristallo* allowed Venetian glassmakers to use threading as the foundation for many original designs. In the sixteenth century, new techniques produced unique and beautiful glassware and the revival of other traditional methods.

Filigree Glass and Other Techniques

Filigree glass used threads and canes as decoration in the ancient world, but it was the Venetians who revived and refined the technique in the sixteenth century. Colorless and opaque white glass canes were embedded in the surface of vessels to create a lacelike effect. Whitehouse explained, "Most filigree glass falls into one of three broad categories: Vetro a fili (glass with threads), which has a pattern of individual stripes; vetro a retor-ti (glass with twisted threads); and vetro a reticello (glass with a netlike pattern of threads)."[51]

Other unique types of glass were developed. Ice glass had a crackled appearance that was accomplished by dipping the hot, colorless glass parison into a bucket of cold water. It was then reheated for additional blowing. Chalcedony glass imitated the semiprecious type of quartz of the same name and was made by melting a mixture of opaque and transparent glass together and adding additional ingredients such as silver nitrate and cobalt oxide.

Venetian glassmakers revived and improved the ancient Roman technique of millefiori glass, which used thin canes of multicolored glass. The prepared patterned glass slices were no longer melted into molds. "Instead," wrote Ricke, "they picked up the disks with a hot gob of glass and subsequently blew them into the shape of a vessel."[52]

The market for glass beads increased, and the Venetians met the demand. These beads were used for church rosaries, in

This cup and basket are examples of delicate, ornamental, Venetian glass called filigree.

jewelry, and as barter goods for the African slave trade and with Native Americans in the New World. Christopher Columbus wrote in his logbook on October 12, 1492: "A large crowd of natives congregated. . . . I presented some of them with red caps and some strings of glass beads which they placed around their necks . . . that delighted them and by which we have got a wonderful hold on their affections."[53]

DO YOU WANT TO KNOW A SECRET?

Most experts agree that Antonio Neri's book, *L'Arte Vetraria (The Art of Glass)*, was the most significant work ever published about glass. Neri was born in Florence in 1576, became a priest, and devoted his life to the study of chemistry. He traveled throughout Italy and Holland and was a scholarly observer at glasshouses in Florence, Murano, and Antwerp.

Neri learned about the manufacture of glass and the various formulas and techniques of glassblowing and decoration. In particular, he carefully studied the styles of the Venetian glassmakers and wrote in detail about all aspects of Venetian glass production.

Neri was apparently unafraid of the Venetian laws that mandated death for anyone who shared Murano glass secrets. Perhaps he felt secure since his early financial patron and supporter was Antonio de Medici, whose wealthy and powerful family controlled much of Florence. The book was dedicated to de Medici when it was published in 1612.

Unfortunately, Neri had little time to enjoy the success of *L'Arte Vetraria*. He died only two years later at the age of thirty-eight. There are no details of where or how he died and very few specifics of his life. However, his contribution to knowledge about glass outlived him. A second edition of the book was printed in Florence in 1661 and a third in Milan in 1817. Editions were also published in English, Latin, German, French, and Spanish.

Secrets Revealed

Venetian glass became the glass of choice for the wealthy and sophisticated Europeans. Glassblowers who fled Murano despite the threat of death received rich rewards and protection in the countries in which they settled. In 1575, a famous glassmaker named Giacomo Verzelini escaped from Italy to London. He was granted a twenty-one-year royal patent from Queen Elizabeth I to make *cristallo* in his own factory and teach English glassworkers the Venetian styles.

In 1612, Antonio Neri, a Florentine priest and chemist, wrote a book called *L'Arte Vetraria* (*The Art of Glass*), in which he revealed formulas and instructions for making a variety of Venetian glasses. It was the first book ever written in detail about the art of glassmaking and was translated and published in England, Holland, Germany, and later in France and Spain. Soon, glasshouses *à la façon de Venise* (in the manner or style of Venice) were built all over Europe.

After the fall of the Venetian republic in 1797, glass production declined, but it was revived again in 1860. Venetian-style glass spread from Europe into America and the New World. Its influence remains significant, even in the twenty-first century.

4

The Spread of Glassmaking: European and American Glass

"[Glass] can be blown into shimmering and ethereal containers or cast into heavy crystalline forms. It can be rough and rugged or polished to pristine perfection. It can appear soft and seductive or jagged and dangerous."

—Karen S. Chambers and Tina Oldknow, *Clearly Inspired: Contemporary Glass and Its Origins*

Additional styles of glass, as well as new techniques of decoration, were developed in response to regional and cultural differences, even as countries continued to strive to produce glassware in the Venetian style. The forest glasshouses of northern Europe used potash to produce the large drinking vessels that were popular in the area. A thicker, less fragile type of crystal was created when Bohemian glassmakers added chalk to the mix. The addition of lead oxide to the glass formula resulted in English lead glass. In America, a new technique was developed in which machines pressed molten lead glass into molds.

Northern European Glass

Waldglas (which means forest glass in German) was made in northern Europe in glasshouses that were conveniently located at the edges of forests so wood could be used as fuel for the furnaces. According to Chloe Zerwick: "The sand contained iron, which produced the typical green color of forest glass. . . . The northern forest glassmaker used wood ashes (potash), which were the natural by-product of his own wood-burning furnace. By carefully purifying the ashes and adding copper oxide, he deliberately nurtured the glossy green hue of the glass."[54]

Zerwick explained that the forest glasshouses were run by secretive guilds, which were very suspicious of outsiders. "Nobody shall teach glassmaking," declared one guild, "to anyone whose father has not known glassmaking. . . . The art may be practiced only by male children [at age twelve] of legitimate marriages within specific glassmaking families."[55]

Large Drinking Glasses

The drinking vessels produced in the forest glasshouses were very large. The most common glass was called a *roemer*, which was used extensively in Germany and throughout Europe during the late sixteenth and early seventeenth centuries. Robert Charleston described it as "a drinking glass . . . with a hollow, cylindrical stem standing on a coiled foot, and with a more or less ovoid bowl rising from the top of the stem. . . . The stem is usually decorated with prunts."[56] The prunts were used to keep a good grip even if the hands were greasy or the person was drunk.

The *humpen* was a very large glass that held several quarts of beer or ale. It was often enameled with patriotic, biblical, or mythological subjects, coats of arms, or even scenes from daily life. A common enameled theme on a *humpen* was the double-headed imperial eagle, which represented the Holy Roman Empire.

A *roemer*, like the one pictured here, was a large drinking glass mostly used by Europeans in the late sixteenth and early seventeenth centuries.

The *passglas* was another large drinking vessel that was passed around from one person to the next. According to art historian Nancy O. Merrill, the *passglas* was "marked with enamel measuring bands placed equidistant on it. As the glass was passed from hand to hand, each drinker had to drink just to the next line on the glass, or, if he missed, he had to drink on to the next line."[57]

Some forest glassmakers had a sense of humor. Charleen K. Edwards described a beaker with portraits of the emperor and empress as well as a "very realistic fly enameled on the bottom, visible [only] when the drinker has drained the glass."[58]

Cut and Engraved Bohemian Glass

In the area of what is now the Czech Republic, Bohemian glassmakers of the seventeenth century developed a new glass more suitable to wheel engraving and stronger than the thin, fragile Venetian *cristallo*. This was done by adding a considerable amount of chalk to the potash glass formula that resulted in a solid, thick-walled, bright, and colorless crystal-type glass.

The cutters and engravers in Bohemia decorated glass vessels in their home workshops. Some became specialists in particular types of designs. Helmut Ricke wrote: "Various artisans, each with a different area of expertise, successively worked on the same glass. . . . The . . . types of cutting were . . . divided up and carried out by different masters. . . . There were engraving specialists for landscape depictions, figures, and decorative applications."[59]

Zerwick noted that Bohemian glasshouses sent traveling cutters and engravers throughout Europe to sell their wares and decorate glass according to the customer's wishes. For a time, Bohemian glass became more popular than Venetian-style glass.

Bohemian Techniques and Technicians

Thick-walled Bohemian glass allowed engravers to use sculptural relief techniques as well as intaglio, in which the decoration

Two kinds of candles were used for lighting in the centuries before the lightbulb was invented in 1879. The cheaper tallow candles were made from the hard, rendered fat of sheep and cattle, and they gave off an unpleasant odor. Wealthier people could afford candles of beeswax, the yellowish substance made by bees in building their honeycombs. Wax candles cost three times more and were heavily taxed, but they had no odor and burned brighter and longer.

Candlesticks were important items in any household. Silver was considered the best candlestick, but those made of English lead glass were nearly as good, since they refracted the light, increasing the brightness. Most homes were very dimly lit, and only on important occasions were a lot of candles used to give off bright light. Even the queen of England kept her quarters dark, using only a few candles. Lit candles were dangerous if not watched closely. The burned wick of both tallow and wax candles had to be trimmed regularly to avoid smoke and fire hazards.

Oil from the sperm whale was used in glass lamps in the first half of the nineteenth century. Despite the bad smell and the small amount of light these lamps provided, sperm oil was the fuel of choice for most Americans until the Civil War. By the 1870s, kerosene for fuel had replaced sperm oil. Glass factories manufactured kerosene lamps, which were safe and inexpensive but required glass chimneys to burn correctly. According to writer Chloe Zerwick, "kerosene lamps were the major home lighting device until Edison developed the electric bulb in 1879."[1] Some kerosene lamps of cut glass sold for several hundred dollars, or, wrote Spillman and Frantz, "twenty times the weekly wage of the craftsmen who did the cutting."[2]

1. Chloe Zerwick, *A Short History of Glass*. New York: Abrams, 1990, p. 80.

2. Jane Shadel Spillman and Susanne K. Frantz, *Masterpieces of American Glass*. New York: Crown, 1990, p. 43.

was deeper, cut below the surface of the glass. A glass engraver named Gottfried Spiller became famous for the combined use of relief carving and intaglio.

In the eighteenth century, a Roman technique in which a design of gold leaf was placed between two layers of glass was revived in Bohemia. A glassmaker named Johann Kunckel developed a new type of ruby-colored glass and ruby-twisted threads that became a decorative specialty of Bohemian glass. Wheel-engraved portrait medallions became very popular, and glass vessels were often decorated with images of rulers.

Bohemian engravers also used sacred themes on glass vessels and reproduced subjects of Renaissance paintings with sculptural relief and deep cutting. After the defeat of French emperor Napoléon Bonaparte in 1815, there was a period of peace in Europe and a renewed growth of the middle class. This resulted in a new, popular style of glass called Biedermeier.

More Is Better

Merrill explained that the nineteenth-century Biedermeier style was "named for verses and drawings of a satirical nature, which lampooned the self-satisfied bourgeoisie [middle class] of a newly conservative Europe."[60] This growing middle class created a new market for lavishly detailed and decorated glass.

Charleston wrote of "a lack of restraint" in Biedermeier glass and the belief that "more of anything could only be good."[61] Despite its over-the-top qualities, Ricke declared that "the themes of the glasses reflect . . . a retreat to the private sphere. Dedications to friends, tokens of love, flower motifs with encoded names, and portraits of family members or of important personalities were popular subjects."[62]

Charleston described a single goblet of this period that had been cut in facets, engraved, stained, jeweled, etched, and enameled. Coats-of-arms decorated both sides of the vessel. An engraving on the front commemorates an important battle. Charleston wrote, "Only gilding is needed to complete the total repertoire of the decorating shop."[63]

The Development of English Lead Glass

Coal began to be used in English glass furnaces after a severe timber shortage resulted in a 1615 law prohibiting the use of wood for fuel. With coal, higher furnace temperatures were reached and glass production costs decreased. An English glassmaker named George Ravenscroft began to experiment with different ingredients, hoping to develop a more sturdy English glass as an alternative to the thin and brittle Venetian-style glass.

Ravenscroft reached an agreement with the Glass Sellers Company of London that provided him with financial support and allowed him to conduct glass experiments in their facilities. At first, Ravenscroft added more potash to the mix, but the glass developed cracks after annealing called crizzling. "Through a substitution of sufficient lead oxide for part of the potash," wrote historians at the Toledo Museum, "he produced a glass that was not only stable, but was soft enough to cut readily without chipping, and of a refractive brilliance never before achieved."[64]

Ravenscroft received a patent in 1674 for the new colorless glass, which was called lead glass. Ravenscroft's agreement with the Glass Sellers Company of London gave them the exclusive right to sell the new glass for the next three years. By 1677, the company used a raven's head seal (from the family's coat of arms) to identify the lead glass of George Ravenscroft. By the late seventeenth century, *waldglas* and Venetian style glass had been replaced in popularity by English lead glass.

Methods of Engraving

Lead glass was particularly suitable for all types of engraving "because of its toughness and brilliance,"[65] wrote Alan MacFarlane and Gerry Martin. Elaborate facet-cutting was popular in English and Irish glassware. A form of diamond-point engraving was developed in Rotterdam, Holland, by a man named Frans Greenwood (1680–1761).

Greenwood was of English descent and used diamond-point stipple engraving to make many light dots on the glass

Glassmakers at work in an eighteenth-century American glass factory.

surface. According to Edwards, "A diamond point, when repeatedly tapped against the surface of glass, produces a pattern of minute fractures which, by refracting light, appear white in contrast to the untouched surface around them."[66]

There was a revival of cameo glass cutting in England by John Northwood (1836–1902), who created a replica of the famous Portland vase in 1876 with opaque white figures on a dark blue background. Controlled acid-etching techniques were also applied in cameo relief designs. Hydrofluoric or sulfuric acid was used to remove the outer glass layer and left the raised design to be cut.

Glass in America

American colonists depended on imported English glass or used wooden or metal drinking cups. The wealthiest owned some Venetian glassware, and English luxury glass was available to those who could pay the price. Writers Jane Shadel Spillman and Susanne K. Frantz wrote that "George Washington ordered glass from England for use at Mt. Vernon, his Virginia plantation. From 1757 to 1773, he ordered 1,200 panes of window

GERMAN ENTREPRENEURS IN AMERICA

Caspar Wistar established a glasshouse in 1739 in Salem County, New Jersey, just south of Philadelphia. He hired German glassmakers to produce window glass, bottles, and tableware. His factory was located near wooded areas and produced greenish glass similar to *waldglas*. Writers Jane Shadel Spillman and Susanne K. Frantz noted that Benjamin Franklin purchased glass tubes from Wistar for use in his electrical experiments. Wistar died in 1752, and his son Richard managed the business until it closed in 1776.

Henry William Stiegel opened a glasshouse in Manheim, Pennsylvania, in 1763 and called it the American Flint Glass Manufactory. He, too, hired German glassmakers to make window glass and bottles. He was also the first in America to produce lead glass tableware in the English style and to compete with imported luxury glass. Stiegel went bankrupt in 1774. The failures of both Wistar and Stiegel were partly caused by the growing political and economic unrest in the colonies prior to the American Revolution.

John Frederick Amelung opened his glass factory in 1784 in Maryland after the war. He called it the New Bremen Glass Manufactory. According to Spillman and Frantz, "he built houses for his workmen near the factory, and a school for their children. . . . This was one of the first planned industrial villages in the United States. . . . Amelung eventually purchased thousands of acres of land to ensure his fuel supply." The business expanded to four glass factories, and at one point, employed five hundred people. This accelerated growth combined with weather-related accidents, fire, and competition from less expensive imported glass drove Amelung into bankruptcy by 1795.

Jane Shadel Spillman and Susanne K. Frantz, *Masterpieces of American Glass*. New York: Crown, 1990, p. 11.

glass, 23 dozen pieces of stemware, 16 decanters . . . and an assortment of other glassware for the table."[67]

The first three successful glassmaking factories in America were all started in the 1700s by German immigrants—Caspar Wistar, Henry William Stiegel, and John Frederick Amelung. All used German workers and produced window glass and bottles in addition to tableware. Wistar and Stiegel were forced to close by the early part of the American Revolution. Amelung's postwar glasshouse opened in 1784, thrived for a time, then went bankrupt in 1795.

The glass industry grew in America along with the country. Since glass was difficult to ship long distances overland without breakage, glassmakers made their way westward along with the pioneers.

The Way West

The first frontier glasshouse opened in 1797 south of Pittsburgh at the junction of the Allegheny and Ohio rivers. The rivers allowed shipping to Virginia, Kentucky, Ohio, and the entire western frontier. The opening of the Erie Canal, which linked Albany with Buffalo, also increased western trade. Soon, additional glasshouses were built along the migration and trade routes as the frontier expanded west to the Mississippi River.

The Louisiana Purchase in 1803 extended American territory from the Mississippi River in the east to the Rocky Mountains in the west, and from the Gulf of Mexico in the south to Canada in the north. In 1800, the U.S. population was 5 million. By 1850, the United States stretched all the way to the Pacific and had a population of 23 million people. Many of these people were middle-class families, and they wanted glassware in their homes.

An early-nineteenth-century traveler wrote, "For want of a glass from which to drink, if you are offered whiskey (which is the principal drink here) the bottle is presented to you or a bowl or a teacup containing the liquor."[68] Whiskey flasks and bottles in standard quantities were mold blown into over six hundred different designs in the mid-nineteenth century.

Many were engraved with patterns and pictures of the American eagle, portraits of George Washington, and national monuments. Other molded glass duplicated the appearance of cut glass.

Making Glass Affordable

In the 1820s, a new process was developed in which molten lead glass was pressed by machines into metal molds. This mechanical pressing allowed for the mass production of tableware and other glass vessels that would now be affordable to the average American family. Glassblowers were not needed, so unskilled workers could be employed, quickly trained, and paid less to supervise the machines. "By the middle of the 19th century," declared Spillman and Frantz, "the pressing process had become so efficient that a team of five men could make 100 tumblers in an hour."[69]

Spillman and Frantz described the difficulties of the mechanical pressing process:

> In order to keep glass from sticking to metal molds and to get a clear impression of the pattern, the molds had to be preheated and then kept at a uniformly high temperature. If the temperature fell much below that of the molten glass . . . it would chill too quickly and the surface would be dull and wrinkled. . . . To mask this problem, the molds were patterned in intricate stippled, "lacy" designs that formed tiny raised lumps on the outside of the glass. Thus, light passing through the glass and reflecting off the stipples distracted the eye from the wrinkled surface.[70]

Many nineteenth-century whiskey bottles, like the ones shown here, were engraved with patterns or pictures of common American symbols.

STAINED-GLASS WINDOWS

In the Middle Ages, the focus of learning centered around churches and monasteries. In Europe, the church promoted the creation of brightly colored stained-glass windows for its large cathedrals. Art historian Charleen K. Edwards wrote that "the monumental works of stained glass by artisans of the Middle Ages are the only notable contributions in an otherwise primitive and rather uncreative glassmaking period. Many of the 12th and 13th century windows are among the greatest artistic and spiritual works of the medieval period."

The Benedictine order of monks saw the use of glass as a way to celebrate God. The large colored windows, the brightness of which changed with greater or lesser sunlight, contrasted with the somber gray cathedral architecture throughout Europe. The windows brought to life religious icons and stories of the Bible. There were twenty-three stained-glass windows in a single cathedral in the Aosta Valley in northern Italy. The subjects included the Madonna and child, the Crucifixion, and Saint Stephen illustrated in vivid colors of red, blue, green, and purple.

Panels of flat glass were colored by the application and firing of various metallic salts, which resulted in the fusion of the metal to the molten glass. Copper salts created a red color, while silver salts created yellow stains on the glass. Color variations and surface alterations such as thickness changed the shading and tone of the window when the light passed through. The glass was cut into shapes and panels of the design. Details were painted directly on the panels with enamel, then the panels were fired and fitted into strips of lead. The completed panels were then all joined together in an iron framework by soldering.

Charleen K. Edwards, *A Survey of Glassmaking from Ancient Egypt to the Present*. Chicago and London: University of Chicago Press, 1977, p. 16.

Whereas only the wealthy could buy expensive matched sets of cut glass, by the mid-nineteenth century most everyone could afford matched sets of pressed-glass tableware. The less expensive the glass, the more likely housewives would purchase additional pieces. A number of New England glassmakers received patents for early pressing machines that varied only slightly from one another. Charleston called Deming Jarves "a leading figure" and "prime mover"[71] in the development of pressed glass. Jarves was head of the Boston and Sandwich Company, and in 1830, he received a patent for a mold in which a handle could be formed with the main body of the piece in one operation.

Three large glass companies in New England became very successful in nineteenth-century pressed-glass production. They were the New England Glass Company, based in East Cambridge, Massachusetts; Jarves's Boston and Sandwich Company in Sandwich, Massachusetts; and the Phoenix Glass Works in Boston. They used each other's techniques and patterns and made such similar pieces that in many cases, it was impossible to distinguish the work of one company from another.

New Developments in Glass

In 1858, John Landis Mason created a special jar for home preserves. The Mason jar was mold blown and the neck and lips were hand finished until the early 1900s, when they were completely made by machine. These containers became very popular and are still used today for home preserving.

In the 1860s, a new formula for a soda-lime glass used in mechanical pressing was developed by William Leighton at a glass company in West Virginia. The new glass was less expensive than lead glass and thinner and lighter, but just as bright. As economic prosperity increased in America, more ornate styles in glass and lighting were developed for those who could afford them. Complex glass pieces were pressed in several sections, and then joined together while the parts were still hot with a thin layer of molten glass.

A social and artistic movement developed in the late nineteenth century in reaction to increased industrialization and

In the late 1800s, new and unusual types of shaded glass were developed. These stylish, decorative art glasses were less expensive than luxury cut glass, but unique and very attractive. A glass called amberina was created by the New England Glass Company. The glass was amber at the bottom and deepened in shade to rose or red at the top.

The addition of small quantities of gold to the glass formula created the amber color, and repeated reheating at the open end resulted in the deeper rose to red colors. Patents were obtained for these new colored-glass formulas that were hand worked, not mechanically pressed. Peachblow was a patented amberina glass lined with a layer of opaque white that made the glass look like porcelain.

The Mt. Washington Glass Company of New Bedford, Massachusetts, created a stained glass called royal flemish. This company also made burmese, which added uranium and gold to the batch that resulted in a pink to yellow color. The intensity and amount of the color depended on the frequency of the reheating process.

mass production in the society. There was a renewed interest in simplistic handcrafted art forms and opposition to classical and historical styles. France became the birthplace of a new period of design called Art Nouveau that changed the worldwide glass movement.

Art Nouveau and Art Deco

"We learned to differentiate original artistic achievements from mass-produced objects, to distinguish what was of genuine value from a mass of trivial products."

—Helmut Ricke, *Glass Art: Reflections of the Centuries*

Art Nouveau (new art) is the term used to describe a movement of decorative and fine arts that emerged in the late nineteenth century. Called *Jugendstil* in Germany, Austria, and Bohemia, it was a reaction against mass-produced, machine-made goods. According to art historian Victor Arwas, "It was an amalgam of influences: Japanese imagery and sensibility . . . the worship of Beauty, admiration for the Arts and Crafts concept of the superiority of the hand over the machine and, above all, the return to Nature, the naturalistic interpretation of flora and fauna."[72]

The sleek, geometric, and abstract style of Art Deco was named after the first international exhibition of decorative arts in Paris in 1925. It was a simple, streamlined style expressive of the machine age. Both Art Nouveau and Art Deco led to an increased involvement by glass artists in the manufacture of their own creations.

All About Gallé

Robert Charleston declared that "Émile Gallé may be considered . . . the artistic mainspring of the Art Nouveau movement in glass."[73] Gallé (1846–1904) was born in Nancy in eastern France. His father owned a shop that produced mirror and table glass, so Gallé learned the glassmaking trade early. He studied art and botany in Germany, London, and Paris before he returned to Nancy and set up his own glass workshop.

Influenced by Japanese art and impressionist paintings, Gallé focused on all aspects of nature and decorated his vessels with flowers, dragonflies, and other insects. He was also inspired by verse and inscribed poetic quotations on some of his vases, calling them *verrerie parlante* (talking glassware).

Émile Gallé is considered by some to be one of the most influential glassmakers in the Art Nouveau movement.

Gallé used multiple layers of colored glass casings in his designs and acid etching to produce floral and other relief. Sometimes the vessel itself was formed in the shape of a flower or plant. Two techniques patented by Gallé in 1898 and often used together were patination and marquetry. Patination produced a rough or smooth matte glass surface after extreme heating. Marquetry consisted of inserting cut pieces of hot, colored glass into the parison and rolling them on the marver to be sure they were embedded in the surface.

Gallé produced varied and original pieces that became so popular other glass manufacturers created pieces in the style of Gallé. The Gallé factories also produced table glass, lamps in floral and fauna designs, including mushroom lamps, and industrial glass. The Gallé glassworks continued production after his death in 1904.

Other Frenchmen, Other Techniques

The Daum Glassworks, operated by the brothers Auguste (1853–1909) and Antonin (1864–1930) Daum in Nancy, developed several new and interesting glassmaking techniques. The first, called vitrification, consisted of a parison of glass rolled over a layer of pulverized colored glass on the marver. After the ground glass was picked up by the hot molten glass of the parison, it was reheated so that the two glass types fused together, resulting in a rough surface. The vessel could be left rough or decorated by etching or polishing. *Verre de jade* (jade glass) and *ceramique de jade* (jade ceramic) were like vitrification, but with a clear glass layer blown over it.

Another Daum process was called the *martelé* effect, which involved wheel-carving the surface of the vessel with tiny,

DEATH, SADNESS, FRUITS, AND VEGETABLES

Émile Gallé produced a wide variety of Art Nouveau glass in the late nineteenth century, ranging in themes from expressive to peculiar. He designed and created a series of black vases for the 1889 Paris International Exhibition. Transparent glass vessels were cased with an outer layer of black or dark brown glass, then carved with themes of death or dying in nature. Other vessels were called vases of sadness, which used a variety of colors and techniques to portray themes of sorrow or melancholy.

Gallé also created cameo vases and glass that imitated hard stones such as amethyst, quartz, jade, and amber. One series of vases had bats as their decoration. Even vegetables and fruits were made into vases and bottles. He designed garlic and corncob vases, and tomato, pumpkin, and artichoke bottles.

faceted cuts, similar to a hammer on metal. The Daums also decorated the inner layer of a vessel by overlaying it with several layers of multicolored glass, resulting in a three-dimensional look. This decoration between the layers is called the intercalary technique and was patented in 1899.

Another Frenchman who designed and made a variety of vessels was François-Eugène Rousseau (1827–1890). Rousseau was highly influenced by Japanese art and styles. "His work was characterized by flame-like colored streaks and contrasting overlays," wrote Zerwick. "Sometimes he added crackle effects and metal particles."[74] Rousseau achieved the streaks and flecks within his glass by embedding metallic oxides between layers of clear glass. The crackling was produced by submerging the hot parison into cold water.

This glass vase by the Daum brothers was made using their intercalary technique.

Pâte de Verre

A method that originated in ancient Egypt was revived by Henri Cros (1840–1907) in the 1880s in France. It was a glass-paste technique called *pâte de verre* and involved grinding glass into a fine powder that was then mixed with metal oxides to provide coloring. The batch was put into a mold and fired in a kiln to fuse the mixture into a solid shape. The temperature was warm enough to melt the paste, but not hot enough to mix the colors together.

Henri Cros produced many soft pastel-colored *pâte de verre* (glass paste) plaques and medallions with a relief decoration using Greek and Roman themes. To achieve the ancient look, he often gave his pieces a rough surface or broken edges.

Other notable artists who worked in the *pâte de verre* style were Albert Dammouse (1848–1926) and Gabriel Argy-Rousseau (1885–1953). Dammouse developed a new enamel glass paste which he called *pâte d'émail*, which was a form of *pâte de verre* that had the appearance of porcelain after firing. Argy-Rousseau used another form of *pâte de verre* that was mixed with ground lead crystal instead of powdered glass. This was called *pâte de cristal* and required a lower temperature when fired.

Glistening Windows, Metallic Iridescence

In the late nineteenth century, Louis Comfort Tiffany (1848–1933) emerged as the creative artistic force in glass in America. The son of the owner of a successful New York jewelry store, the wealthy Tiffany studied painting in Paris. He established his own New York glasshouse in Corona, Long Island, and by 1885 had started the Tiffany Glass Company.

Tiffany began to produce leaded glass windows with a colleague named John La Farge. Tiffany incorporated the landscapes of America into his window glass subjects and created them using only colored glass and lead, not paint or stain. According to Charleston, the "windows . . . were literally pictures painted in glass and light. . . . La Farge and Tiffany developed new types of glass . . . suggesting drapery folds, foliage and rippling water. They also made extensive use of milky opalescent glass . . . helping to create the effect of a painting rather than of a window."[75] Tiffany began producing leaded lampshades in the style of his windows. The lamps were very expensive, and most had floral designs. The lamps were very popular, in part because the milky glass gave a warm glow to the light.

Tiffany's decorated luster glass (patented in 1880) was produced by applying chunks of colored glass to the surface of a vessel and then combing it with metal tools to form various

This *pâte de verre* plaque by Henri Cros features the Greek goddess Circe.

patterns. The applied decoration took on "a metallic luster" in contrast to the rest of the piece, after immersing it in a wash of metallic oxides or "by exposing it to vapors or gases."[76]

Tiffany wanted to go beyond luster glass and achieve the iridescent look of ancient glass that had been buried underground for hundreds of years. His chemists developed iridescent, opaque colors that could be used in the production of hand-blown vessels. This process became synonymous with the Tiffany name. The result was blown glass, entirely furnace made, in flower, feather, or stem designs with a glowing metallic iridescence.

In the late nineteenth century Louis Comfort Tiffany emerged as the foremost glassmaker in America.

Favrile Glass

With business booming, Tiffany decided on a trademark name, Favrile, in 1894 to describe all glass created by his company. He produced floral-form vases, tableware, and cypriote glass that simulated the look of ancient buried glass, complete with a pitted surface and sometimes surface bubbles.

Lava glass had a rough and grainy surface and was meant to resemble a volcanic eruption, with gold-colored lava lumps that were made by adding basalt or talc onto the parison. Tiffany also produced gooseneck vases and reactive glass that changed color when reheated.

After World War I (1914–1918), Tiffany split up his company and stopped creating original designs, although the company continued to assemble lead glass windows and shades. The Art Nouveau style was fading by the 1920s, and Tiffany closed down the glasshouse on Long Island.

Carder and Steuben Glass

Frederick Carder (1863–1963) at Steuben Glass provided the main competition for Tiffany's Favrile glass. Carder, whose father was a potter, designed glass for the English firm of Stevens and Williams for fourteen years. In 1903, he emigrated to America and began Steuben Glass Works in Corning, New York. Although his main job was to supply undecorated blanks for cutting, Carder began experimenting with glass in unusual colors and shapes from nature. He developed a new iridescent glass he called Aurene (one of many he created), which was an iridescent gold or blue glass with threaded and floral patterns.

In 1918, Corning Glass Works bought Steuben Glass Works, but Carder continued as managing director and then art director until the 1930s. Over the years, he created a large variety of glass in exotic colors. Carder produced *rouge flambé*, a bright red glass that consisted of selenium, cadmium sulfate, and chromium oxide. *Verre de soie* was a silky, iridescent glass produced by spraying the surface with a solution of stannous chloride. Ivrene was an opaque white glass with a luster decoration that made it look like an iridescent pearl.

Carder retired in 1936 but continued to design glass into the 1950s using a small kiln in his workshop studio at Steuben. He

Blown glass vases by Frederick Carder. Carder was considered Louis Comfort Tiffany's main competitor.

often used the *cire perdue* (lost-wax) technique for his original sculptures. This process required a wax model covered in plaster, which hardened to form a mold. When this was heated, the wax melted and drained out through openings in the base, leaving the mold. When molten glass was poured into the mold, the glass assumed the shape of the original wax model. After annealing, the mold was broken to reveal the finished work. Carder continued to work in glass into his nineties.

Sleek and Streamlined Art Deco

A new artistic style emerged in the 1920s and 1930s. Called Art Deco, it exalted the machine age and emphasized simplicity of line, geometric designs, and abstract and stylized forms. "It's so . . . evocative of the so-called streamline feeling," declared glass artist Dan Dailey, "which suggests motion, suggests the future, suggests speed."[77]

Glass doors designed by René Lalique for an exhibition of glass at the Brever Galleries.

René Lalique (1860–1945) was a very successful and well-known maker of fine jewelry before he turned to glass. He purchased his first glass-house in 1908 in Combs-la-Ville, France, to fill orders to design and produce high-quality perfume bottles for fragrance manufacturers. He bought his second, larger glass factory in 1918 in Wingen-sur-Moder, France.

Lalique produced mold-blown glass, pressed glass, and sometimes used the *cire perdue* method for individual works. He created a wide range of glass articles, including large wall dressings, decorative panels, doors, and illuminated fountains. He also designed and produced glass panels and lighting for ocean liners, restaurants, and churches.

René Lalique's series of automobile hood ornaments were perfect examples of the Art Deco style in glass. As cars became faster, sleeker in design, and more expensive, car mascots, which fit on the front hood, became a significant feature of the total automobile package. Lalique created hood ornaments that lit up and changed colors when the car was moving, the effect of which was especially impressive at night.

His most famous hood ornament was called *Victory or Spirit of the Wind*. It is a woman's head in glass, mouth and eyes wide open, leaning forward, with a mass of what art historian Victor Arwas described as "geometrically aligned hair streaming back" from the face. Other popular car mascots designed by Lalique included a dragonfly, horses' heads, a greyhound, a falcon, and an eagle's head, which, Arwas noted, was much sought after by officers of Adolph Hitler's Nazi party to attach to their vehicles.

Hood ornament by René Lalique on a 1932 Delage D8S coupe.

Victor Arwas, *Glass: Art Nouveau to Art Deco*. New York: Abrams, 1987, p. 190.

Lalique worked mostly with clear, uncolored glass or opalescent glass, which had a milky shine and bluish tint to it. Some of his early works were in the Art Nouveau style, but his later pieces "are more characteristically Art Deco," wrote Arwas, "with geometric friezes of birds, figures or plants, rigorously zig zag patterns in both shape and decoration."[78] He used contrasting high-relief ornamentation and deep, beveled designs on many of his glass vessels, and he developed a process of surface coloring that darkened and highlighted the exterior patterns.

Inspired by the Glass Itself

Whereas most glass artists created the designs and supervised the blowing of the glass by a team of skilled workers, Maurice Marinot (1882–1960) learned to blow and shape the molten glass himself. "Marinot was probably the first man in the Western world to undertake the making of glass single-handed,"[79] wrote Charleston. Originally a painter, he first became fascinated with glass in 1911 when he visited a small glasshouse owned by friends.

Marinot became determined to create glass art himself, and his friends allowed him to use the factory at night and at lunch breaks. At first, he experimented with enameling pieces made from his own designs. He used bright blues and reds to enamel birds, flowers, and figures on vases, decanters, and other bottles. Despite receiving critical acclaim for his work, he was dissatisfied with merely creating surface decoration. He wanted to make the molten glass vessels himself.

Marinot practiced day after day and slowly learned the skills of blowing and shaping molten glass. He worked by himself or with one assistant. According to Arwas, Marinot produced two basic styles of glass, "One a smooth-surfaced vessel in various shapes trapping colors and patterns within its very thick walls, the other equally thick-walled but with its surface deeply cut or etched in abstract patterns."[80]

In 1937, the factory closed and the internationally acclaimed glass artist had no choice but to return to painting. Art historian Martha Drexler Lynn declared that Marinot "bridged the

A glass chalice made by Maurice Marinot, one of the first men in the Western world to make glass himself without using a team of skilled workers.

divide between artistic vision and the ability to execute it. . . . He imputed a spiritual character to the activity of forming glass and he believed that art made of glass had to come directly from the hands of the artist."[81]

The Modernist Movement

Orrefors Glasbruk of Sweden became the first glass company specifically to hire artists to design glass and work directly with factory craftspeople. Painters Simon Gate (1883–1945) and Edward Hald (1883–1980) were employed in 1915 and 1917 to work with Orrefors master glassblower Knut Bergqvist (1873–1953) creating new designs.

Gate and Bergqvist developed a new decorative technique called graal glass in which a colored layer of glass of a cut or etched relief design was then reheated and covered with another layer of clear glass. Then the piece was blown out into its final

QUEZAL ART GLASS: A TIFFANY RIVAL

Two former Tiffany employees, Martin Bach Sr., a glass chemist, and Thomas Johnson, a glassblower, joined together to create the Quezal Art Glass and Decorating Company in 1902 in Maspeth, Queens, New York. Quezal offered new and different iridescent glass in the Art Nouveau style to compete with Tiffany.

Writer Malcolm Neil MacNeil described Quezal glass as "vases, compotes, drinking vessels, and shades for lighting fixtures . . . often fashioned to resemble flowers, such as crocuses, tulips, or lilies. Variously colored inlaid threads or veins of glass, pulled and twisted by hooks, simulate naturalistic floral or leaf patterns and vines." According to MacNeil, "Opal, gold and green colors prevail and the glass is generally opaque. Compared with Tiffany's Favrile glass, the crisp, vivid, and colorful decoration of Quezal art glass is distinctively precise, symmetrical, and restrained."

The company was named after a Central American bird with brilliant feathers of iridescent green and deep purplish red. By 1924, most of the skilled artists and craftspeople had moved on to other glass manufacturers, although the company was not officially dissolved until 1948.

Malcolm Neil MacNeil, "Quezal Art Glass," *Magazine Antiques*, January 1998, p. 186.

form and finished, resulting in a smooth outer surface over an expanded inner relief decoration. In addition to decorative glass, Gate and Hald also produced elegant, simple, and functional tableware that inspired American glass manufacturers.

In the twentieth century, the German Bauhaus style of functional art and architecture was characterized by severe geometric designs and simplicity of forms, frequently using glass as building material. Architects like Walter Gropius and Ludwig

Mies van der Rohe emigrated to the United States to escape the Nazis and "changed the face of American cities with their glass-walled houses and skyscrapers,"[82] wrote Jane Shadel Spillman and Susanne K. Frantz.

The Road to Studio Glass

Gallé, Tiffany, and Lalique all owned their own glass factories. They sketched original designs and supervised the execution of pieces by a glassmaking team. The three never actually worked at the furnace themselves like Marinot (although Lalique worked with *cire perdue* glass).

Other artists like Gate and Hald were hired by large factories to design glassware, and the work was carried out by the glassblowing team, not the designers themselves, who oversaw the work. There was only one artist who blew glass outside of the factory setting. Jean Sala (1895–1976), a Spaniard living in France, maintained a small studio with a self-made furnace and worked with molten glass during the 1930s and 1940s.

An American artist named Harvey Littleton visited Sala in 1958 and saw pictures of his small furnace with an annealing oven on top. After meeting Sala and making a trip to the glasshouses in Murano, Littleton became convinced that glass could be blown by individual artists in small studios. He returned to America, determined to pursue this quest.

The Studio Glass Movement

"Strongly held was the belief that glass could not be blown by less than the traditional six-man blowing team of the pre-industrial revolution shop."

—Susanne K. Frantz, *Contemporary Glass: A World Survey from the Corning Museum of Glass*

Established factories dominated the glass industry in the years after World War II (1939–1945). Hundreds of employees mass-produced glass objects daily, each assigned a single task in the multiphased process. Although some individual designers and factory owners created original and unique glass pieces, it was Harvey Littleton, Dominick Labino, and their students who were the catalysts for the studio glass movement. Glassmaking changed from a skilled craft in a factory to a studio environment in which artists working alone produced original pieces of expressive art.

House Designers, Guest Artists

Glasshouses such as Steuben in New York, Waterford in Ireland, and Baccarat in France became world renowned for their pure and brilliant lead crystal glass. In-house designers created tableware, cut glass, and small sculptures, and glassmaking teams produced the pieces.

Some companies began the practice of commissioning individuals outside of the company to produce new glass designs. In the 1940s, Steuben invited artists to design more abstract pieces, breaking from their previously distinctive style of heavy, rounded and engraved glassware. Since then, Steuben sculpture has been equally as important as the company's tableware.

Martha Drexler Lynn wrote, "Factory attitudes fostered contempt for those who tried to be amateur glassworkers."[83] As late as 1947, Steuben designer Sidney Waugh declared, "Glassblowing . . . is not within the scope of . . . even the most talented artist or craftsman working alone."[84]

Pre-Studio Innovators

Prior to the studio glass movement of the 1960s, several notable glass artists developed unique and interesting techniques and designs, and they are considered forerunners of the studio glass movement. Paolo Venini (1895–1959) had a law practice in Milan, Italy, when he teamed with Giacoma Cappellin (1887–1968) and produced simple, colorless, or pastel-colored

A handkerchief vase by Paolo Venini and Fulvio Bianconi.

glass with no outer decorations. Arwas wrote that these "were a startling contrast" to the "over-decorated glass for tourists that was being turned out"[85] at that time in Murano.

Venini opened his own factory in 1925. He designed his own pieces but also hired outside designers to create new styles. He developed several new glassmaking techniques, but his most famous creation was the handkerchief vase that he collaborated on with Fulvio Bianconi in 1946. It became a very popular piece and was made in a large variety of colors and surface textures. By the 1960s, the factory had invited many well-known outside artists to design for them, including the famous painter Salvador Dali. Although Venini died in 1959, his factory in Murano is still one of the largest and most successful today.

Frances Higgins (1912–2004) and Michael Higgins (1908–1999) designed and created glass together for more than fifty years. They met at the Chicago Institute of Design and married in 1948. Working independently, they reintroduced and perfected the technique of fusing crushed or flat glass in kilns. *American Craft Magazine* wrote, "Their technique involved coating sheets of window glass with color enamels and slumping the layers of enameled glass over a shallow mold in a kiln."[86]

The Higginses were also "known for their brightly colored, geometric-patterned glass enamel tableware"[87] wrote Lynn, which they created for department stores like Marshall Field and Bloomingdale's. After 1966, the two concentrated solely on studio work. Frances created vessels made with fused clear glass that resembled crushed ice. The tops of the pieces were purposely left uneven so it looked like the ice was melting. Michael made hinged boxes of fused glass with copper joints and metal bands.

Monumental Glass Sculpture

A married team of glass artists from Czechoslovakia became pioneers in creating large glass sculpture as architecture. The first prominent piece by Stanislav Libensky (1921–2002) and Jaroslava Brychtova (1924–) was displayed in the Czech pavilion of the World's Fair in Brussels, Belgium, in 1958 and consisted of concrete walls embedded with cast-glass animal designs.

Toshichi Iwata (1893–1980) is considered a pioneer of the glass industry in Japan. He studied oil painting and sculpture at the prestigious Tokyo Art School and became interested in glass after seeing an exhibit by the Daum brothers of France. High-quality glass was scarce in Japan and generally imported by the wealthy, who could afford it.

Iwata opened his own factory in the 1930s and trained his workers through a process of trial and error. For Iwata, glass was just another expressive medium, similar to painting and sculpture. Although he was head designer at the factory, he hired additional in-house workers to create new shapes, forms, and patterns in glass. Iwata's work often reflected oriental themes of beauty and art.

Libensky and Brychtova used the technique of internal hollow modeling that highlighted the interior light and features of the cast glass, a sculptural effect only possible with glass. They created a huge glass installation for the opening of a new Corning Museum of Glass building in 1980 called *Meteor, Flower, Dove.*

According to Chloe Zerwick, "the meteor incorporates the logo of the Corning Glass Center, thus representing Corning as a glassmaking nucleus; the bird in flight stands for worldwide communication between glassmakers; and the flower suggests the eternal beauty of glass."[88]

Infatuated with Glass

Harvey Littleton (1922–) was always passionate about molten glass. He was born in Corning, New York. His father worked at Corning Glass Works, he took art classes at the Corning Free

Academy, and he worked summers at Corning, inspecting blown-glass cookware and making molds.

After serving in World War II, Littleton completed an industrial design degree from the University of Michigan and then a master of fine arts from Cranbrook Academy of Art in Bloomfield Hills, Michigan. He worked as a potter and taught ceramics from 1949 to 1951 at the Toledo Museum of Art School of Design. In 1951, Littleton accepted a position at the University of Wisconsin in Madison and focused on clay until 1957, when he traveled to Paris and Murano.

Back home in Wisconsin, Littleton wrote, "I took upon myself the challenge to try to develop the techniques necessary for a person to work alone as an artist in glass."[89] In 1962, Toledo Museum director Otto Wittmann agreed to sponsor two glass-making seminars on the grounds of the museum. These two workshops took place on March 23 to April 1 and June 18 through June 30. Many art historians point to these dates as the beginning of the American studio glass movement.

Labino and the Workshops

Dominick Labino (1910–1987) first teamed with Littleton when Littleton taught ceramics at the Toledo Museum. Labino was the vice president and director of research at Johns-Manville Fiber Glass Corporation. An electrical engineer by training, Labino was knowledgeable about glass chemistry and even experimented with glassblowing using a small home furnace he had built himself.

Labino was extremely interested in the workshops and offered advice to participants on building small, inexpensive furnaces for affordable home studios. He also furnished number 475 glass marbles, used by Johns-Manville to make fiberglass, that were easily melted down and used for exploratory glassblowing. By the second workshop, each student tried to complete a simple blown object, and educational possibilities in glass at the college and university level were also discussed.

Interest in glassmaking surged after an article profiling Littleton appeared in *Life* magazine and the publication of the

Glass Workshop Report. In 1962, Littleton was further influenced by a trip to Europe and his meeting with German glass artist Erwin Eisch. Helmut Ricke wrote: "Like no other European glass artist he [Eisch] rejected the traditional glass vessel outright. . . . An opaque usually deep black glass melt became his material of choice. . . . Glass became a sculptural medium."[90]

Littleton taught a class in glassblowing at Wisconsin in the fall of 1963. It was the first course in glasswork ever offered at an American university for credit. That same year, the Art Institute of Chicago opened an exhibit of his studio glass. Littleton's students and followers became an expanding network throughout the country, creating original artwork, receiving museum recognition, and teaching classes in glass as members of the faculty at various colleges and universities.

A Split in the Movement

Littleton believed only the solitary person who worked with hot glass and practiced free blowing was a true studio artist. He felt the focus of the movement should be the expressive content of the art itself and shifted away from vessels to sculptural forms.

Dale Chihuly poses next to one of his glass sculptures at the Fairchild Tropical Botanic Garden in Coral Gables, Florida, in 2006.

Labino, on the other hand, believed the focus should be on technique. "To understand glass, one should know its properties—chemical and physical. There are many unexplored combinations both in composition and in colorants,"[91] declared Labino. He devoted most of his life to extensive study and research and received sixty patents for his glass formulas, glass-related devices, and furnace designs.

By the 1980s, the definition of studio glass had changed to include all artists who worked outside of the factory in any glass technique—warm (slumping, fusing, *pâte de verre*, and kiln forming), cold (cutting, engraving, painting, and polishing), and hot (free blowing, mold blowing, and casting).

Littleton's Pupils Take Center Stage

Marvin Lipofsky (1938–) was one of Littleton's first students of glassmaking at the University of Wisconsin, where he received a master of fine arts degree. In 1964, he began the second college glass program in the country, teaching courses at the University of California, Berkeley, until 1972. Lipofsky also initiated the glass department at the California College of Arts and Crafts in Oakland, where he taught until 1987.

Throughout the 1970s and 1980s, he traveled in Europe and Asia, experimenting and collaborating on glass sculpture with factory blowers. According to Jane Shadel Spillman and Susanne K. Frantz: "This artist has always approached glass as a medium for his abstract forms. . . . Some of Lipofsky's early pieces are covered with paint or textural materials that deny the translucency and reflection of the glass, forcing the viewer to heed the form instead."[92] Lipofsky also worked with mold-blown organic shapes, which were then modified with cold-working techniques.

The most commercially successful and widely known of those who studied with Littleton at the University of Wisconsin is Dale Chihuly (1941–). After earning a degree in interior design from the University of Washington, he studied glassblowing with Littleton in 1966. He received a master of science degree in 1967 from Wisconsin and a master of fine arts from the Rhode Island School of Design in 1968, where he established a glass department there the following year.

An American in Venice

In 1968, Chihuly, the recipient of a Fulbright scholarship, became the first American glassblower actually to work at the famous Venini factory in Murano, not just observe or design. He learned the Venetian style of glass, and this experience influenced him in two later series, *Seaforms*, which he began in 1980, and *Venetians*, which he began in 1988.

Describing *Seaforms*, Chambers and Oldknow wrote, "Chihuly pushes to an extreme the delicacy that characterizes this work, with sensuous forms, pale colors, and surface patterrings reminiscent of Venetian decorative techniques . . . the undulating rim of a Chihuly vessel in which the glass has been pulled out during the final forming shows an affinity [close resemblance] with the Venini handkerchief bowls of the late 1940s and 1950s."[93]

In 1976, Chihuly's life and his work in glass changed. He lost the vision in his left eye after a car accident, and he could no longer safely work with molten glass by himself. Chihuly began to paint or sketch his ideas and concepts for new glassworks and closely directed a handpicked team of glassmakers to produce the completed piece, similar to the Italian method. His experiences helped to redefine and broaden the definition of a studio artist.

Gold Chandelier, 1998, by Dale Chihuly hangs above a staircase in Benaroya Hall in Seattle, Washington.

A Significant Body of Work

Chihuly created a Basket Cylinders series that combined blown cylinders decorated with glass thread drawings based on the designs of American Indian blankets. His Pilchuck basket series was inspired by designs of northwest coastal Indian baskets. A series called Macchia combined basket and sea forms into one.

By the 1990s, Chihuly was creating large outdoor installations all over the world, from Jerusalem and Japan to Las Vegas and Tacoma, Washington, where he was born. His 20-foot-high chandeliers (6m) sometimes consisted of thousands of glass

THIS TRAILBLAZER MELTED GLASS IN HER BASEMENT

Ohio ceramist Edris Eckhardt (1910–1998) began to experiment with melting glass in her home basement studio in 1953 because she wanted to reproduce Roman gold glass. This ancient technique involved a gold (or silver) leaf design that was inserted between two layers of transparent glass. Working without scientific training and using her electric ceramics kiln, she managed to make her own glass from raw materials, then colored the glass with oxides.

Eckhardt "used wet wooden rolling pins to flatten the crude sheets of glass on a marble slab. These sheets would then be covered with gold or silver leaf, engraved or drawn upon with under glazes and glass enamels, fired, and annealed, then sandwiched with other layers and fused," explained art historian Susanne K. Frantz.

Eckhardt also created glass sculpture using the *cire perdue*, or lost-wax, technique similar to Frederick Carder's. Her small piece entitled *Archangel* was, according to Frantz, "the only attempt by an American artist to produce glass sculpture in a hot state to be included in The Corning Museum of Glass exhibition, 'Glass 1959.'"

Susanne K. Frantz, *Contemporary Glass: A World Survey from the Corning Museum of Glass*. New York: Abrams, 1989, p. 36.

pieces. Writer Tracy Zollinger Turner declared, "Chihuly's designs are more like wild, oversized sea anemones or patches of coral reefs that might exist in some marine version of Alice's Wonderland."[94] In 2002, Chihuly's Bridge of Glass opened in Tacoma. It is a 500-by-20-foot bridge (152m by 6m) that crosses over a main highway and connects to the city's waterfront. The bridge also features many examples of Chihuly sculpture.

"The term 'fantastic' can be applied to Dale Chihuly's entire body of work," wrote art historians Rosa Barovier Mentasti and Maurizio Sciaccaluga. "In his own inimitable way, he plays with the most provocative colors, creating breathtaking compositions that catch the light in cunning ways."[95]

Following Labino's Lead

One of the earliest studio glass artists to follow Dominick Labino's focus on glass chemistry and technique was Chicago-born Mark Peiser (1938–). In 1961, he received a degree in product design from the Illinois Institute of Technology. He worked in business and took music classes at DePaul University. In the summer of 1967, he attended the Penland School in North Carolina and took two courses in glassblowing. He became so interested in the glassblowing process that within several months, he became a Penland artist in residence and operated the first one-man glass studio.

All of Peiser's pieces were created from his own experimentation with glass and color formulations. Among Peiser's early works were highly decorated miniature vases with a metallic luster and larger vessels with an opaque background.

In 1975, Peiser created a series called Paperweight Vases that utilized the interior of the vessel for patterns and designs. Spillman and Frantz wrote: "[These] Paperweight Vases . . . were built up by applying glass canes heated by a torch between successive layers of colorless glass. The process is a difficult one since all decorating and forming of the vessel must be completed while the glass is still molten."[96] Peiser had to sit by the furnace and work the glass for six to eighteen hours straight before a piece was completed.

THE PILCHUCK SCHOOL

ounded by Dale Chihuly and others in 1971, the Pilchuck Glass School began as a summer workshop and evolved into a world-famous center of glass arts located north of Seattle, Washington. "It brings together small groups of students and a renowned international faculty for concentrated sessions in all glass working methods," wrote glass expert Robert J. Charleston. "Pilchuck's informal atmosphere and its open-minded philosophy regarding the potential of glass as an artistic medium has made the school a magnet both for established artists interested in incorporating glass in their work and for students from around the world." Many contemporary glass artists of today have spent time in residence at the Pilchuck Glass School.

Robert J. Charleston, *Masterpieces of Glass: A World History from the Corning Museum of Glass.* New York: Abrams, 1990, p. 231.

The Spread of Studio Glass

The bond established between Littleton and Eisch in 1962 helped to spread the concept of studio-made glass to Europe, Japan, and the rest of the world. Glass artists began to focus more on content and ideas than technique. Iridescent glass was revived, and sandblasting became a popular method of surface decoration. Many artists avoided vessel shapes or covered the glass entirely in paints or metallics. Glass was frequently fused with other material.

Top museums in the country began actively to seek out studio glass for their exhibits. The Corning Museum of Glass, which opened in 1951, sponsored Glass 1959, which was important in encouraging early participants in the studio glass movement. In 1979, the Corning Museum sponsored New Glass: A

Worldwide Survey, which traveled throughout America, Europe, and Japan. Susanna K. Frantz declared that this exhibition had "a significant influence on the future of contemporary glass. . . . [It] was the first opportunity for artists, educators, curators, collectors, art dealers, and the general public to see the most up-to-date assortment of this still new phenomenon."[97]

Since the 1979 Survey exhibition, there have been numerous other exhibitions, increased educational programs, and a growing number of artists using many new, unusual, and interesting approaches to glass. Frantz concluded, "The most recent years of studio glass have . . . firmly established [it] as a legitimate medium for the artist."[98]

Contemporary Glass

"Glass became a sculptural medium. . . . It allowed the artist to tell stories, to address emotions and compulsions . . . the artist purposely invited controversy."

—Helmut Ricke, *Glass Art: Reflections of the Centuries*

By the early twenty-first century, glass had evolved into a recognized art form. It offers infinite possibilities to the contemporary artist through the use of a variety of traditional and nontraditional materials and techniques without restrictions on size or subject matter. "The artist may transform a personal vision," wrote Chloe Zerwick, "into a statement of universal meaning expressed in terms of transparency and light."[99]

Ancient Images and Harmony with Nature

William Morris (1957–) was only twenty years old when he got a job as a truck driver for the Pilchuck Glass School in Stanwood, Washington. He was so fascinated by glass that he learned glassblowing and eventually became an instructor at the school beginning in 1979. He worked with Dale Chihuly as head gaffer (leader of a glassblowing team) for many years in the late 1970s and early 1980s before establishing his own studio.

Morris's early work focused on primitive handmade objects and prehistoric drawings and rock carvings. His subject matter has included prehistoric mastodons, birds, bison, horses, panthers, and other animals in realistic forms. One of his large glass installations, called *Cache*, is 36 feet (11m) long and consists of an enormous animal skeleton made of more than one hundred glass elephant tusks tied together. Inside the structure are skulls, bones, and primitive tools that look real, but are made entirely of glass. Art historian James Yood wrote of Morris, "His technical skills are simply astounding; his ability to make blown glass appear as bone, skin, bronze, leather, clay, metal, and more is so accomplished that it might appear effortless."[100]

In his early work, William Morris focused on primitive objects like these Egyptian canopic jars featuring elk heads.

A 2001 series of his sculptures deals with the human body and its decorations, including facial art, tattoos, jewelry, head-dresses, and accessories such as spears, feathers, shields, beads, necklaces, pots, and tools. These pieces were the first by Morris to concentrate on the human figure. He chose to highlight a diversity of people, including Native American, African, Asian, Arabic, and other figures, portraying them at their cultural peak as part of the family of man.

According to Yood, Morris believes "there was once a time and a place and a range of cultures more in harmony with nature, with the rhythms of this planet, than anything he can discover around him today. He seeks that time and place, and in his art he finds it, and offers it to us."[101]

Filet de Verre

Toots Zynsky (1951–) first became intrigued with glass in 1969 at the Rhode Island School of Design when she was eighteen years old. Two years later, she helped Dale Chihuly form the Pilchuck Glass School in the state of Washington. Zynsky received her bachelor of fine arts degree from Rhode Island in 1973. She then began experimenting with glass threads that she pulled by hand and individually fused with blown-glass forms.

By late 1982, Zynsky collaborated with a friend and colleague to design and build a thread-pulling machine. This allowed her to create larger quantities of longer, multicolored glass threads. Soon she began to create vessels completely made from intertwined strands of thousands of glass threads, eliminating the blown glass completely. Zynsky called this new technique *filet de verre* (French for "net of glass"). In 1983, Zynsky designed a series of *filet de verre* vessels for the Venini Company in Italy.

Robert Charleston described the *filet de verre* technique:

> Zynsky transforms heated rods of various colors into uniform thread. Cooled lengths are arranged, fused in a two-stage kiln-firing process, and then warmed until they sag into a bowl-shaped mold. The artist reaches

into the kiln [with heatproof gloves] to manipulate the rim into soft folds while the bowl is still hot. Zynsky's works are pure glass. . . . The color is that of the glass, not paint, and no changes are made in the piece once it is removed from the kiln.[102]

Karen S. Chambers and Tina Oldknow wrote, "The resulting 'vessels' are like brushstrokes of color frozen forever in space and time."[103]

Inspired by what Chambers and Oldknow referred to as the "fusion of both rich and muted tones"[104] in Italian paintings of the fourteenth and fifteenth centuries, Zynsky uses dynamic and luminous colors to create beautiful objects. "Some vessels are autumnal, with vibrant hues of orange, gold and brown," declared writer Eleanor Heartney. "Others make one think of the pale greens, yellows and flashes of red in early spring. The riotous combinations of scarlet, blue-purple and emerald in some recall the brilliance of tropical birds and fish. Colors lie in patches that meld into each other at their feathery edges."[105]

Monumental Vertical Glass

Large glass sculpture has been the focus of the work of Howard Ben Tre (1949–), a graduate of the Rhode Island School of Design in the late 1970s. He originally worked in metal, then applied the same casting techniques to glass, but on a larger scale. Ben Tre works with poured glass, not blown, producing sculptures that may stand 12 feet (4m) high and weigh up to 1,200 pounds (544kg). Many of his pieces contain granite or gold accents and bands of lead, brass, and copper.

Ben Tre starts out with detailed drawings, then produces a three-dimensional Styrofoam model, which is then transformed into a sand-filled metal mold. According to writer Jonathan Goodman:

Ben Tre casts sculptures once each year at a glass factory; the molds, which contain between 300 pounds and 2,000 pounds of molten glass, must cool for 2½ months before they can be opened. Minor faults in the glass surface—pocks and fissures—are embraced by the artist, who sees the imperfections as allowing light to penetrate the form. Ben Tre finishes the work by hand, often coating the concavities with color or gold leaf.[106]

REPRODUCING ROMAN CAGE CUPS

Etsuko Nishi (1955–) was born in Kobe, Japan, but lives and works in London. She attended the Pilchuck Glass School in the 1980s and has a doctorate degree from the Royal College of Art in London. Her focus in glass has been on the qualities of softness embodied in such fabrics as silk and lace in the form of vessels that are brilliantly formed. Nishi was inspired by a *pâte de verre* (glass paste) cup by Albert Dammouse that she viewed at a museum in Paris. The small cup was "made from extremely thin and delicate glass," explained Nishi, "and shaped to imitate purple, pale pink, and pale yellow petals. It was titled *Anemone* and looked most beautifully soft and delicate."[1] Nishi was determined to reproduce her own version of the Roman cage cup and Chambers and Oldknow described the process she used:

> To create a lacy enclosure attached by struts . . . she casts the interior vessel, then wraps it with fireproof batting, and inserts the glass struts. Using a pastry tube filled with a paste of glass, she "connects the dots," drawing what will be the outer cage. The piece is then heated and the struts are fused to both the inner and the outer forms. The batting . . . withstands the heat of the kiln but dissolves in water after the piece is cooled. . . . Nishi's exquisite castings look as delicate as spun sugar.[2]

1. Quoted in Karen S. Chambers and Tina Oldknow, *Clearly Inspired: Contemporary Glass and Its Origins.* Maldon, England: Pomegranate, 1999, p. 76.

2. Chambers and Oldknow, *Clearly Inspired*, p. 37.

The importance of his sculpture is in the meaning or connection the viewer can get from the piece. "Howard Ben Tre wants you to do this: Touch it, sit on it, walk around it. Above all, don't worry about what it means. It means . . . whatever response it evokes in you,"[107] declared writer Gloria Goodale. Ben Tre stated: "I hope that the sculpture is going to have a lot of layers of meaning. But I hope that people without any history of looking at art, can be drawn in, and have a connection to it."[108]

Beginning in the late 1990s, Ben Tre focused on outdoor sculpture using water. Over the course of a decade he created five glass-and-bronze columns with a water dome in a New York park, and he has designed benches, fountains, planters, streets, and plazas in cities such as Boston, Providence, Minneapolis, and Warrington, England. Ben Tre explained that the purpose of his public art and bringing his work out of the galleries is in "elevating the consciousness of those who view and use it."[109]

Functional Vessels into Nonfunctional Works of Art

A unique and original method of working with glass has been developed by Jay Musler (1949–). He focuses on the surface until the transparent and reflective qualities are completely obscured with paint. According to James Yood, "Musler's elements —we really should call them characters—-huddle together in compositions of great tenderness, little vignettes that suggest a narrative we can't fully decode. . . . Musler's elements are never human but always are human in some parallel universe where our hopes and fears and desires find full play."[110]

Musler attended the California College of Arts and Crafts from 1968 to 1971, then took a job blowing traditional, functional glass at a northern California art glass company. He attended a conference at the Corning Museum of Glass in the late 1970s and became aware of the modern Swedish glass of the 1920s. He declared: "The Swedish vessels made me think of glass as a vehicle of expression. In fact, they helped me to find my voice in art."[111]

In 1981, Musler left his job to pursue a career in glass and create individual works. Writer Melinda Levine wrote that Musler "defies the limits of glass, pushing it so far that it loses the characteristics that traditionally define it: reflection, gloss and transparency."[112] Musler works with both small, nonfunctional vessels as well as large panels, masks, and detached standing screens. The glass form is just the beginning of the process for Musler, who first sandblasts the glass, taking away the shine, then paints the glass in unique oil colors.

"No one works in the range of greens, yellows, and oranges that he does," wrote Yood. "Musler's is the work you immediately recognize from dozens of yards away, pungent and assertive, unexpected and completely his own. His works almost seem to radiate light, to glow from some fire within, every bit as hard won as the glass on which it resides."[113]

One of his most famous pieces is *Cityscape* (1981), a bowl shape with the rim cut like an urban skyline. Charleston wrote:

> He chose a purchased piece of Pyrex glass, made for laboratory or commercial use. The container was cut down to form a hemispherical shape, its skyline rim notched by high-pressure sandblasting. Musler . . . rendered the bowl nonfunctional in a traditional sense by airbrushing oil paint on the interior and exterior surfaces to suggest the effect of an urban community bathed in the deceptively beautiful orange glow of dust, grime, and pollution.[114]

Quirky Irreverence

The humorous and often satirical irreverence for conventional art forms has been an ongoing characteristic of the work of Richard Marquis (1945–). He received a bachelor of arts degree from the University of California, Berkeley, in 1969, where he was influenced by the Pop Art and Funk movements that often used comic book illustration and everyday imagery of soup cans, soda bottles, and other objects as an expression of art. After graduation, Marquis earned a scholarship to study in Italy and worked

Ohioan Doug Anderson (1952–) was inspired by the *pâte de verre* (glass paste) technique of nineteenth-century French artists and reproduced it in his work sometimes in conjunction with the *cire perdue* (lost-wax) technique. Anderson looked to nature for his subject matter, and several of his best-known pieces use actual fish and other real objects. Karen S. Chambers and Tina Oldknow wrote, "Stimulated by the rural Ohio setting in which he was living . . . he was intrigued by the delicacy of the scales of the bluegills in a pond near his home, noticing that details he might miss in real life observation appeared when cast."[1]

In *Fish Bowl* (1982), a small fish sits in the middle of the bowl. The mold was formed around the fish, cast in wax, and then fastened to a wax mold of the bowl. According to Spillman and Frantz, Anderson then "packed . . . mold material around the wax, which, when dried, was heated, melting out the wax and leaving a cavity. The mold was filled with crushed, colored glasses that were fired slowly, then cooled over a period of days. Later, the mold was broken away, freeing the glass vessel."[2]

Other Anderson pieces include *Fish Plate* (1985), which consists of thirteen fish connected together in a circle, and *Finders Creepers* (1986), a single piece of glass which illustrates a section of a forest floor. Frantz wrote, "It incorporates 15 different types of flora and fauna cast from life, including ivy leaves, an apple leaf, vine, snake, peanut, button, cicada, horsefly, pine cone, two feathers, . . . mushrooms, acorns, strawberries, rocks, and black-eyed Susans."[3]

1. Karen S. Chambers and Tina Oldknow, *Clearly Inspired: Contemporary Glass and Its Origins.* Maldon, England: Pomegranate, 1999, p. 41.

2. Jane Shadel Spillman and Susanne K. Frantz, *Masterpieces of American Glass.* New York: Crown, 1990, p. 75.

3. Susanne K. Frantz, *Contemporary Glass: A World Survey from the Corning Museum of Glass.* New York: Abrams, 1989, p. 237.

at the Venini factory. He returned to the United States in 1970 and earned a master of arts degree from Berkeley in 1972.

For much of his career, Marquis has used the murrine technique in combination with other materials and objects. This is similar to the mosaic and millefiori processes in which "different colors of glass [are] fused together in bundles to form a design and then heated and drawn out to reduce the size of the cane," explained Chambers and Oldknow. "Slices of this cane are used to decorate or form objects."[115] Whereas millefiori glass used the pattern of a thousand flowers, Chambers and Oldknow wrote that Marquis developed his own murrine designs, "everything from hearts to skulls to the Lord's Prayer—and used them to form the bodies of his comically misshapen teapots."[116] Writer Maria Porges declared, "Works like his Teapot Goblets, Teapot

Maya Lin has utilized recycled glass in many of her major works of art.

Trophies and Teapot Tripods . . . place a homey, traditional vessel in some very unexpected situations."[117]

In 1979, Marquis produced the Fabricated Weird series, one of which is called *Potato Landscape Pitcher*. It consists of a brown blown-glass potato with cane protrusions extending outward, sitting on a sand-filled paperweight base. On top of the potato is a small pitcher with a white spout on which is written, "Chuck the duck/says life is/mostly hard work."[118] Marquis often finishes a serious sculpture with ceramic toys, plastic dice, rubber ducks, or other silly objects embedded on the top.

"Mr. Marquis does not follow any particular rules or styles,"[119] declared a 1995 Wignall Museum/Gallery catalog. "He has created a varied and weird body of work,"[120] stated a Glass Art Society Annual Conference brochure. When Marquis received the 2005 Glass Art Society Honorary Lifetime Achievement Award, Oldknow said, "His prolific body of astonishingly original, challenging, and exquisitely executed work illustrates his boundless range and exceptional versatility as an artist."[121] Art critic Regina Hackett wrote: "While Dale Chihuly is the tide that raised all boats, Marquis is the craft intelligence that made the vessels seaworthy. He taught the second generation of American glass artists that skill extends freedom instead of limiting it."[122]

Recycled and Broken Glass

The technique of integrating recycled glass as well as natural or living materials into the work was utilized by sculptor and architect Maya Lin (1959–). Lin was only twenty-one and a senior at Yale University majoring in architecture when her entry for the Vietnam War Memorial was chosen in 1980. She began to focus on the landscape and the environment in the 1990s. *Groundswell* is a 1993 sculptural landscape she created for the Wexner Center for the Arts at Ohio State University. It is a tri-level garden that consists of 40 tons (36,287kg) of crushed, recycled green glass shaped into wavy mounds and valleys. Lin explained: "It's about a meeting of East and West. It's a play on the Japanese raked gardens of Kyoto, as well as the Indian burial and effigy mounds of Athens, Ohio . . . but it's also about bringing a studio artwork mentality out of doors."[123]

Avalanche, created by Lin in 1998, is another major work composed entirely of recycled glass. It measures 10 feet (3m) by 19 feet (5.8m) by 21 feet (6.4m) and consists of 11 tons (9,979kg) of greenish-blue glass. According to the PBS series *Art in the Twenty-First Century*, Lin's *Avalanche*

> is an essentially abstract work that makes connections between man-made materials and patterns naturally occurring in nature . . . the work seems to leak out from the gallery corner and onto the floor. . . . The glass itself is glittery and seductive, tempting the viewer to reach out and grab a dangerous handful. Occasionally and without warning, tremors will send small avalanches of glass rumbling down the surface.[124]

Since its discovery, glass has been defined and discussed in terms of its function, culture, artistic movement, and production method. That is no longer the case. Modern glass has evolved into pure artistic expression that has no limitations or boundaries. If there is one characteristic of contemporary art in glass, it is diversity—of form, of artists, of materials, and of methods.

Notes

Introduction: The Evolution of Glass

1. Dominick Labino, *Visual Art in Glass*. Dubuque, IA: Brown, 1968, p. ix.
2. Labino, *Visual Art in Glass*, p. 6.
3. Alan MacFarlane and Gerry Martin, *Glass: A World History*. Chicago: University of Chicago Press, 2002, p. 188.

Chapter One: Ancient Origins

4. Mary Luella Trowbridge, *Philological Studies in Ancient Glass*. Urbana: University of Illinois Press, 1930, p. 194.
5. Pliny the Elder, *Natural History*. New York and London: Penguin, 1991, p. 392.
6. J.R. Vavra, *5,000 Years of Glassmaking*. Prague, Czechoslovakia: Artia, 1954, p. 16.
7. Labino, *Visual Art in Glass*, p. x.
8. Frederic Neuburg, *Glass in Antiquity*. London: Art Trade, 1949, p. 9.
9. Toledo Museum of Art, *Art in Glass*. Toledo, OH: Toledo Museum of Art, 1969, pp. 13–14.
10. Toledo Museum of Art, *Art in Glass*, pp. 13–14.
11. Chloe Zerwick, *A Short History of Glass*. New York: Abrams, 1990, p. 18.
12. Robert J. Charleston, *Masterpieces of Glass: A World History from the Corning Museum of Glass*. New York: Abrams, 1990, p. 32.
13. Toledo Museum of Art, *Art in Glass*, p. 14.
14. Zerwick, *A Short History of Glass*, p. 17.
15. Zerwick, *A Short History of Glass*, p. 12.
16. Trowbridge, *Philological Studies*, p. 103.
17. Trowbridge, *Philological Studies*, p. 194.

Chapter Two: Roman Glass and the Discovery of Glassblowing

18. Quoted in Homer L. Hoyt, *Glassblowing*. Golden, CO: Crafts & Arts, 1989, p. 6.
19. Toledo Museum of Art, *Art in Glass*, p. 21.
20. Charleston, *Masterpieces of Glass*, p. 51.
21. MacFarlane and Martin, *Glass*, p. 13.
22. Quoted in Corning Museum of Glass, *Glass from the Ancient World*. Corning, NY: Corning Museum of Glass, 1957, p. 67.
23. Quoted in Corning Museum of Glass, *Glass from the Ancient World*, p. 69.
24. Karen S. Chambers and Tina Oldknow, *Clearly Inspired: Contemporary*

Glass and Its Origins. Maldon, England: Pomegranate, 1999, p. 16.

25. Quoted in Charleston, *Masterpieces of Glass*, p. 44.

26. Pliny the Elder, *Natural History*, p. 363.

27. MacFarlane and Martin, *Glass*, p. 14.

28. Charleston, *Masterpieces of Glass*, p. 35.

29. Robin Brooks, *The Portland Vase*. New York: HarperCollins, 2004, p. 4.

30. Chambers and Oldknow, *Clearly Inspired*, p. 18.

31. Zerwick, *A Short History of Glass*, pp. 28–32.

32. Neuburg, *Glass in Antiquity*, p. 15.

33. Charleston, *Masterpieces of Glass*, p. 40.

34. Quoted in Zerwick, *A Short History of Glass*, p. 32.

35. Pliny the Elder, *Natural History*, p. 357.

36. Charleen K. Edwards, *A Survey of Glassmaking from Ancient Egypt to the Present*. Chicago and London: University of Chicago Press, 1977, pp. 6–7.

Chapter Three: The Spread of Glassmaking: Middle Eastern and Venetian Glass

37. Zerwick, *A Short History of Glass*, p. 32.

38. Helmut Ricke, *Glass Art: Reflections of the Centuries*. Munich, Berlin, and London: Prestel Verlag, 2002, p. 36.

39. Toledo Museum of Art, *Art in Glass*, p. 35.

40. Charleston, *Masterpieces of Glass*, p. 72.

41. Chambers and Oldknow, *Clearly Inspired*, p. 18.

42. Zerwick, *A Short History of Glass*, p. 48.

43. Edwards, *A Survey of Glassmaking*, p. 16.

44. Zerwick, *A Short History of Glass*, p. 50.

45. David Whitehouse, "European Glass in the Venetian Style, 1500–1750," *Magazine Antiques*, August 2004.

46. Chambers and Oldknow, *Clearly Inspired*, p. 22.

47. MacFarlane and Martin, *Glass*, p. 21.

48. Quoted in Charleston, *Masterpieces of Glass*, p. 99.

49. Charleston, *Masterpieces of Glass*, p. 84.

50. Ricke, *Glass Art*, p. 369.

51. Whitehouse, "European Glass in the Venetian Style, 1500–1750."

52. Ricke, *Glass Art*, p. 78.

53. Quoted in Zerwick, *A Short History of Glass*, p. 51.

Chapter Four: The Spread of Glassmaking: European and American Glass

54. Zerwick, *A Short History of Glass*, p. 59.

55. Zerwick, *A Short History of Glass*, p. 58.

56. Charleston, *Masterpieces of Glass*, p. 112.

57. Nancy O. Merrill, *A Concise History of Glass*. Norfolk, VA: Chrysler Museum, 1987, p. 27.

58. Edwards, *A Survey of Glassmaking from Ancient Egypt to the Present*, p. 26.

59. Ricke, *Glass Art*, p. 88.

60. Merrill, *A Concise History of Glass*, p. 38.

61. Charleston, *Masterpieces of Glass*, p. 176.

62. Ricke, *Glass Art*, p. 110.

63. Charleston, *Masterpieces of Glass*, p. 176.

64. Toledo Museum of Art, *Art in Glass*, p. 57.
65. MacFarlane and Martin, *Glass*, p. 25.
66. Edwards, *A Survey of Glassmaking from Ancient Egypt to the Present*, p. 34.
67. Jane Shadel Spillman and Susanne K. Frantz, *Masterpieces of American Glass*. New York: Crown, 1990, p. 3.
68. Quoted in Charleston, *Masterpieces of Glass*, p. 188.
69. Spillman and Frantz, *Masterpieces of American Glass*, p. 35.
70. Spillman and Frantz, *Masterpieces of American Glass*, p. 31.
71. Charleston, *Masterpieces of Glass*, p. 195.

Chapter Five: Art Nouveau and Art Deco

72. Victor Arwas, *The Art of Glass*. Windsor, Great Britain: Andreas Papadakis, 1996, p. 19.
73. Charleston, *Masterpieces of Glass*, p. 204.
74. Zerwick, *A Short History of Glass*, p. 94.
75. Charleston, *Masterpieces of Glass*, p. 227.
76. Quoted in Charleston, *Masterpieces of Glass*, p. 208.
77. Quoted in Chambers and Oldknow, *Clearly Inspired*, p. 58.
78. Victor Arwas, *Glass: Art Nouveau to Art Deco*. New York: Abrams, 1987, p. 189.
79. Charleston, *Masterpieces of Glass*, p. 220.
80. Arwas, *The Art of Glass*, p. 67.
81. Martha Drexler Lynn, *American Studio Glass*, 1960–1990. New York: Hudson Hills, 2004, p. 30.
82. Spillman and Frantz, *Masterpieces of American Glass*, p. 60.

Chapter Six: The Studio Glass Movement

83. Lynn, *American Studio Glass*, p. 27.
84. Quoted in Lynn, *American Studio Glass*, p. 27.
85. Arwas, *Glass*, p. 345.
86. *American Craft Magazine*, June/July 1999, p. 24.
87. Lynn, *American Studio Glass*, p. 39.
88. Zerwick, *A Short History of Glass*, p. 111.
89. Harvey Littleton, *Glassblowing: A Search for Form*. New York: Van Nostrand Reinhold, 1971, p. 8.
90. Ricke, *Glass Art*, p. 257.
91. Labino, *Visual Art in Glass*, p. 117.
92. Spillman and Frantz, *Masterpieces of American Glass*, p. 67.
93. Chambers and Oldknow, *Clearly Inspired*, pp. 34–35.
94. Tracy Zollinger Turner, "Dale Chihuly: Godfather of Glass," *Dialogue*, November/December 1998, p. 24.
95. Rosa Barovier Mentasti, Rosanna Mollo, Patrizia Framarin, Maurizio Sciaccaluga, Anna Geotti, *Glass Throughout Time*. Milan, Italy: Skira Editors, 2003, p. 143.
96. Spillman and Frantz, *Masterpieces of American Glass*, p. 74.
97. Susanne K. Frantz, *Contemporary Glass: A World Survey from the Corning Museum of Glass*. New York: Abrams, 1989, p. 159.
98. Frantz, *Contemporary Glass*, p. 207.

Chapter Seven: Contemporary Glass

99. Zerwick, *A Short History of Glass*, p. 111.
100. Quoted in Blake Edgar and James Yood, *William Morris: Man Adorned*.

Seattle: Marquand in association with the University of Washington Press, 2001, p. 26.

101. Edgar and Yood, *William Morris*, p. 29.
102. Charleston, *Masterpieces of Glass*, p. 236.
103. Chambers and Oldknow, *Clearly Inspired*, p. 39.
104. Chambers and Oldknow, *Clearly Inspired*, p. 96.
105. Eleanor Heartney, *American Craft Magazine*, February/March 1999, p. 112.
106. Jonathan Goodman, *Art in America*, April 2002, p. 145.
107. Gloria Goodale, "Artist Forms Meaning in Poured Glass," *Christian Science Monitor*, February 18, 2000, p. 20.
108. Quoted in Goodale, "Artist Forms Meaning in Poured Glass," p. 20.
109. Quoted in Robert Silberman, "Howard Ben Tre: Interior/Exterior," *American Craft Magazine*, April/May 2000, p. 48.
110. Quoted in Marx-Saunders Gallery, "Jay Musler." www.marxsaunders. com/guide/featured.image.index.iht ml?step=2&startnum=1&maxval ue=9&c=14&n=289&o=1&incre ment=9.
111. Quoted in Melinda Levine, "Jay Musler," *American Craft Magazine*, April/May 2003, p. 40.
112. Levine, "Jay Musler," p. 40.
113. Quoted in Marx-Saunders Gallery, "Jay Musler."
114. Charleston, *Masterpieces of Glass*, p. 228.
115. Chambers and Oldknow, *Clearly Inspired*, p. 133.
116. Chambers and Oldknow, *Clearly Inspired*, p. 39.
117. Maria Porges, "Richard Marquis: Material Culture," *American Craft Magazine*, December 1995, p. 36.
118. Quoted in Frantz, *Contemporary Glass*, p. 111.
119. Quoted in Richard Marquis, "Propaganda: Biographical Sketches." www.richardmarquis.com/index.php ?page=biographical_sketches.
120. Quoted in Richard Marquis, "Propaganda: Biographical Sketches."
121. Quoted in Richard Marquis, "Propaganda: Quotes." www.richardmar quis.com/index.php?page=quotes.
122. Quoted in Richard Marquis, "Propaganda: Quotes."
123. Quoted in PBS, "Art 21: Art in the Twenty-First Century: The Series—Maya Lin." www.pbs.org/art21/ artists/lin/clip1.html.
124. Quoted in PBS, "Art 21: Art in the Twenty-First Century: The Series—Maya Lin."

Glossary

abstract: Nonrepresentational expressions of forms or objects.

alkali: Any of various bases that neutralize acids.

anemone: A cylindrical-shaped form of marine life with flowerlike tentacles at the top; sea anemone.

anneal: To cool gradually so as to reduce stress and prevent cracking.

art glass: Glass that is made for ornamental rather than functional use, intended for display purposes.

batting: Cotton, wool, or other fibers used in padding.

beveled: Adjacent surfaces carved on glass surfaces that do not form right angles; slanted or sloping.

blank: Any shape of glass that requires further forming, finishing, or decoration.

blowpipe: A long metal tube used to blow molten glass.

bourgeoisie: Middle class.

canes: Rods of glass.

cased glass: A thin layer of glass over another layer of glass of a different color.

crizzling: A glass defect that causes lines and cracks in the glass surface and dull-ness; also sometimes used as a decorative technique.

cuneiform: Wedge-shaped characters used in writing by ancient Assyrians, Babylonians, Persians, and others.

decanter: Ornamental glass vessel for holding wine or brandy.

ductile: Able to be molded or shaped; malleable.

embellishment: Ornamentation added to enhance beauty.

ethereal: Light, delicate.

fire: Subject to heat; bake in a kiln.

gilded: Coated with gold or gold leaf.

glaze: The smooth, glossy surface or coating on ceramics.

intaglio: A type of engraving in which the decoration is cut deeper, below the surface of the glass.

inundated: Flooded, deluged.

irreverence: Lack of respect.

kiln: A furnace or oven for burning, baking, or drying.

kiln forming: Shaping glass in a mold by heating it in the kiln just enough to melt it into the desired shape.

lathe: A machine that holds or rotates a piece of glass or metal against a shaping tool.

malleable: Able to be molded or shaped; ductile.

marver: A flat work surface of stone or iron on which the glass is rolled to smooth and shape it.

molten: Liquefied by heat.

nonporous: Not able to be penetrated by water or liquid.

opaque: Dull and cloudy; not allowing light to pass through.

parison: A lump or mass of molten glass; also called a gather.

patrician: A person of high class or rank.

pontil: The iron rod that is attached to the parison.

potash: Wood ashes.

pristine: Pure; in its original state.

prunts: Thornlike protrusions in glass.

refraction: Direction of light rays.

relief: Raised surface or projection.

sandblasting: A decorative process in which a glass piece is bombarded with grains of sand to produce various effects such as a frosted, matte surface or actual cuts.

slumping: The process of heating glass until it softens and sags into the shape of a specific form or mold; also referred to as molded or cast glass.

soda: Sodium carbonate used mainly in the manufacture of glass.

solder: A metal mixture that can fuse and join other metal objects together.

stipple: A type of engraving that uses dots on the glass surface.

strut: A brace or support.

studio glass: Designed and made by an independent artist instead of a glassmaker in a factory.

stylized: Distinct characteristics that represent a specific form or design.

tumbler: A stemless drinking glass with a flat bottom.

undulating: Wavy form.

utilitarian: Useful and practical.

vitrification: The process in which substances fuse together at a certain temperature and become glass.

Books

Corning Museum of Glass, *A Guide to the Collections*. Corning, NY: Corning Museum of Glass, 2001. Excellent illustrations in this museum overview.

Ruth Kassinger, *Glass: From Cinderella's Slippers to Fiber Optics*. Brookfield, CT: Twenty-First Century, 2003. This book describes the characteristics of glass, techniques of glassmaking, and the uses of glass throughout history.

Harvey Littleton, *Glassblowing: A Search for Form*. New York: Van Nostrand Reinhold, 1971. Excellent large and detailed illustrations of the glassblowing process.

Tina Oldknow, *Richard Marquis Objects*. Seattle: Seattle Art Museum, 1997. An illustrated look at Marquis's whimsical and humorous glass sculpture.

Jane Shadel Spillman and Susanne K. Frantz, *Masterpieces of American Glass*. New York: Crown, 1990. This book focuses on American glass from colonial times to the present.

William Warmus, *The Essential Dale Chihuly*. Seattle: Seattle Art Museum, 1997. Everything you ever wanted to know about Chihuly and his work with glass, with excellent illustrations.

Chloe Zerwick, *A Short History of Glass*. New York: Abrams, 1990. This is an interesting, well-written history with good illustrations.

Web Sites

Dale Chihuly (www.dalechihuly.com). This site includes DVDs and videos of the artist and his work.

The Corning Museum of Glass Educational Site (www.cmog.org). This site offers a variety of resources and information about art in glass.

Glasslinks Guide to the History of Glass (www.glasslinks.com/history.htm). Many different and interesting links to glass-related subjects.

Richard Marquis (www.richardmarquis.com). This site includes the artist's latest works and exhibits.

National American Glass Club (www.glassclub.org/glasssi.htm). Numerous links to glass organizations and associations, general glass topics, glass factories, museums, and workshops.

Index

Picture Credits

About the Author

Phyllis Raybin Emert is the author of forty-six books on a wide variety of subjects—from animals and automobiles to unsolved mysteries and women in the Civil War. This is her first title for Lucent Books. She lives in northern New Jersey with her husband, Larry, and has two grown children.